AN EXTRAORDINARY
SACRIFICE

THE STORY OF PC NICOLA HUGHES, 16.10.1988 – 18.9.2012

BRYN HUGHES

To Christine Seider
Thanks for your support

Bryn X

AN EXTRAORDINARY
SACRIFICE

THE STORY OF PC NICOLA HUGHES, 16.10.1988 – 18.9.2012

BRYN HUGHES

MEREO
Cirencester

Mereo Books

1A The Wool Market Dyer Street Cirencester Gloucestershire GL7 2PR
An imprint of Memoirs Publishing www.mereobooks.com

An extraordinary sacrifice: 978-1-86151-397-7

First published in Great Britain in 2015
by Mereo Books, an imprint of Memoirs Publishing

The address for Memoirs Publishing Group Limited can be found at
www.memoirspublishing.com

The Memoirs Publishing Group Ltd Reg. No. 7834348

The Memoirs Publishing Group supports both The Forest Stewardship Council® (FSC®)
and the PEFC® leading international forest-certification organisations. Our books
carrying both the FSC label and the PEFC® and are printed on FSC®-certified paper.
FSC® is the only forest-certification scheme supported by the leading environmental
organisations including Greenpeace. Our paper procurement policy can be found at
www.memoirspublishing.com/environment

Typeset in 11/15pt Plantin
by Wiltshire Associates Publisher Services Ltd. Printed and bound in Great Britain by
Printondemand-Worldwide, Peterborough PE2 6XD

CONTENTS

Foreword
Introduction
Acknowledgements

FOREWORD

For most of us losing a loved one is the most traumatic and distressing time in our lives, a feeling of helplessness, of remorse, of regret for not doing or saying the things that we wanted to do or say.

Most bereaved people cling to the ledge of hope, that time will heal most of the pain and that rational thought will eventually replace the emotions of irrational musings, allowing the mind, soul and body to recover and to discover a new way of living without the person who made your life complete, worthwhile and whole.

Of the pain and sorrow I have experienced in my 49 years of life, I would subscribe wholeheartedly to the above statements, give or take a few moments of weakness, but to have the most precious thing in the world that you have taken from you in the most brutal, callous and public of ways, leaves me cold and wondering how on earth the families of PCs Nicola Hughes and Fiona Bone, gunned down in cold blood just because of the uniform that they wore and the values that they held, make sense of all the clichés, proverbs, and 'it will get easier' comments?

I know Bryn Hughes, the father of PC Nicola Hughes, very well. I know his family well too, but it is with deep regret and sadness that I know him and that I know his family in the way that I do. I wish I had never met Bryn Hughes, or his family - I wish that Bryn Hughes was just an ordinary man who I would pass in the street and think nothing of, an ordinary man who I would glance across at in a traffic jam and forget in an instant. But Bryn Hughes is not an ordinary man, he is the father of PC

Nicola Hughes, one of two officers under my command, who was lured to her death and murdered in the most calculated and inhumane way possible.

In this book Bryn talks about the love and the life that Nicola gave to him and her family and of the support that she gave to the countless others who were blessed with having met or worked with Nicola. He talks about the moments after he learned of his daughter's murder as well as the weeks, months and years beyond - his life sentence.

When most other people would understandably withdraw from society, Bryn Hughes was determined not to allow his daughter's death to have been in vain, and he is now determined to turn horror into hope for so many others.

I was extremely privileged to have known Nicola Hughes, to have served with her in the finest police service in the world. I am equally proud to know Bryn Hughes - no ordinary man, no ordinary story.

Nick Adderley
Chief Superintendent, Greater Manchester Police

INTRODUCTION

On the morning of September 18 2012, my daughter Nicola Hughes was on duty as a police officer with Greater Manchester Police. On that morning she was paired up with a colleague from her relief, PC Fiona Bone. During the morning they were asked to attend an address in Hattersley, near Hyde, where a caller had reported that someone had thrown a concrete slab through his window. When they arrived, they were confronted by a wanted criminal with a gun, who immediately opened fire on them with an automatic handgun with an extended magazine, shooting them both dead in cold blood. The call had been a trap, laid with the sole purpose of killing one or more police officers.

When the news was announced, the nation went into shock. My life and the lives of my family and others close to Nicola changed, in the blink of an eye, forever that day.

I have written this book to tell the story of what happened, and as a tribute to my beautiful young daughter.

Bryn Hughes
February 2016

ACKNOWLEDGEMENTS

My sincere thanks to the following, whose great help
has made this book possible:

Nat Hughes, my wife and Nicola's step-mum, for
her understanding, her support, her contribution and
at times, criticism.

John Scheerhout of the *Manchester Evening News*,
for allowing me to quote from his book about the crime,
Lured To Their Deaths.

Stephen Mann, Chief Executive at Police Mutual
Assurance, for the support and use of their offices
(special thanks to Sue and Dawn).

Many rank and file members of the Police Service
for words of comfort at the most difficult times.

To my good friends Mark Brook, Kenny Mortin,
Mark Hanson, Duncan Hutchinson and Richard and Lauren
Bartlett, who have helped, listened and been patient.

My ex-Governor Susan Howard, for words of wisdom
and support in those early days.

To Richard Donovan for supporting our ongoing
fundraising efforts.

CHAPTER 1

'The best of both of us'

I remember the day Nicola was born as if it were yesterday. It all started on a Saturday night, October 15 1988. Nicola's mum, my former wife Sue, went into labour at one o'clock on the Sunday morning; I hadn't been to bed as I had been caretaking my late father's social club in Oldham that night.

Nicola finally popped out just before lunchtime on the Sunday, at 12.21, in the maternity ward at the Royal Oldham Hospital. I had been up all night, so by then I hadn't slept a wink for well over 24 hours, but I didn't feel in the least bit tired – just weeks before my 25th birthday I had become a father. I was on a real high.

There were a few complications with the birth when Nicola was giving up the fight due to complications. Her heart actually stopped a couple of times, so it was quite an ordeal for Sue and me. When Nicola was resuscitated she was placed in what looked like a fish tank with blankets and a heater; in fact I helped the hospital staff to dismantle the bed in the delivery suite.

She weighed in at 6lb 2oz and she seemed so tiny - I suppose when it's your first child you just don't realise how small they are. I was overwhelmed by the whole thing and very emotional, though I'm not usually an emotional person. I was excited at being a father, but it was also quite frightening to know that I was responsible for a little life. I was only 24 and I'd never had any real responsibilities before. I can remember saying to myself, 'Time to grow up now'. I had to go straight back to work - there was no paternity leave then.

When the hospital photographer came round to take Nicola's picture, my little girl didn't look too pleased about it. She had dark hair and was looking cross and moody, as if she was thinking, 'What do you think you're playing at, dressing me up like this?' I thought what a strong-minded little thing she seemed, even at a few hours old - I was right about that, as it turned out.

As for me, I was born on November 2 1963, and grew up in Oldham, Lancashire, my late father's side coming from Llangollen in North Wales, while my mother's side were from Oldham and the Isle of Man. I was the second of three brothers - the older one is Graham and the younger one is Kevin.

I had a happy and secure childhood for the first nine years or so, but unfortunately my parents then split up. My dad was an electrician who worked away in Scotland a lot - I don't know if that had anything to do with the break. We stayed with Mum of course and Dad was happy with the single life. My Father, Jack, died 14 years ago aged just 59, but Joy, my mum, is still around - she's well into her seventies now.

I was an active as a child and played a lot of football, usually a disorganised game with 25 per side on the school field, though I wasn't particularly skilled.

My old school had its own swimming pool where you could 'enjoy' swimming and canoeing, not something I particularly liked, not being a strong swimmer. I did enjoy the outdoor pursuits option later. We never excelled academically, but we were all strong and active and as fit as fiddles due to 'playing out' for as long as we could until it went dark or we became hungry.

After school we would go around the streets in home-made 'bogeys' we would make with any scraps of wood we could find. The steering mechanism was made from washing line, which we had probably nicked or borrowed from someone's line, and a hole was burnt through the wood with a red hot poker - we had possibly pioneered the first cordless drill, but we didn't know it.

My first job after I left school was at Tesco in the warehouse, until I fell down the steps and broke my wrist after the Christmas party. We would fill a new dustbin (off the shelf) with as much booze as we could, er, find, in the warehouse and drink it as you would do from a punchbowl.

After a period on the sick I decided Tesco wasn't the place for me and started work as a gravedigger, would you believe, working for the local council in the graveyard of a big church in Saddleworth. I only stuck it for about three months. It always seemed to be cold and wet, and apart from that the work was simply boring.

I met Sue, Nicola's mum, in the local pub. We were friends due to her interest in our local karate club. We married in May 1987 after seeing each other for a short time. I was just 23 and Sue was slightly older at 24.

By this time, after a couple of other jobs, I was working as a sandblaster, which was a good line to be in as there were a lot of rebuilding and regeneration projects going on. For a couple of years I was working in Albert Dock in Liverpool, where there was a huge regeneration project going on and all the old brickwork had to be cleaned up. I also worked on social housing projects.

I didn't see sandblasting as a long-term career however, as it can be unpredictable and of course it's seasonal. My then wife's stepfather worked at Strangeways as a prison officer, and from what he told me it sounded like an interesting job and one with security, prospects and a pension at the end of it. That was quite an attraction to me after all the other jobs I'd done.

I was more or less talked into applying. I attended an interview with a selection board and sat an entrance exam, which I managed to pass. Recruitment then was done on a national basis and there was a national shortfall of prison officers.

I attended Prison Service College for nine weeks in Wakefield, which at the time was an hour's drive from home. I would return to the training college every Monday morning at 6 am. We only had one car at this time, so we would strap Nicola into the child seat and drive over the M62 to Wakefield. I'd wave goodbye and then not see her for a week at a time.

Halfway through training we received our postings. I thought with having a wife and family I would be staying in the north - how wrong was I! I opened my letter and read, 'HMP Grendon'. I looked at the map and worked my finger down from Oldham and eventually found it, slap bang in the middle of Buckinghamshire. I was to work there for just over two years, living away from home in the 'hostel' or section house. There were 26 of us, paying just £10 a month for a single room.

It was very satisfying to feel I was embarking on a secure career. Nicola was two years old by now and as a young family man I felt a great sense of responsibility. Twelve months before I had been single and living at home with my mum, and now I had a wife and baby to care for.

The time I spent on my own was difficult being away from home. Back in 1991, mobile phones were a thing of the future, except for the rich and famous. Ordinary people like me would queue at the call box with the other officers and take it in turns to ring home. Depending on the time when I rang home I would speak to Nicola, and she would always ask 'when are coming home Daddy?' I would spend around 10 days at work and come home for a long weekend.

By the time I had made my way home on the train it was late on Friday night, so I wouldn't see Nicola until the following morning. Then it was time to get ready to travel back on Monday. I felt extremely guilty about not being there for her for those two years and missed so much of the way she was growing and developing into the little girl she was.

When Nicola was born we were living in a two up, two down terraced house in Oldham, but within a few months we had moved to a three-bedroom semi on the east side of Oldham. We had bought a series of Disney books for Nicola, and although she was unable to read them herself, I would choose a different book each night and start to read the story to her in the hope that she would soon drift off to sleep. However, Nicola would stay awake for most of the story, by which time I had fallen asleep on her bed. She would then get out of bed, go downstairs to her mum and tell her, 'Dad's fallen asleep again'.

Nicola's brother Sam was born in 1992. That was another complicated birth, but he was a fit baby and soon grew into a happy and healthy child. When Nicola was nine and Sam was five we moved to a much bigger house in Saddleworth, a four-bedroom semi in the village of Diggle, the village that was to become her home for the remainder of her short life.

Nicola went to Hey with Zion Primary in Oldham, then Diggle Primary School, before going on to Saddleworth High School. She loved school and rarely missed a day and was always up out of bed very early to get ready. She even liked doing her homework. She always took great pride in her studies.

Nicola and I had a great relationship as she grew up, and it was wonderful to see the way her personality developed. She was always full of fun, and as soon as she could walk she used to enjoy rough and tumble. Although she was fit and active she didn't particularly focus on one sport at school. I would always 'play fight' with both Nicola and Sam. She had this knack of being able to climb on top of you and pin your legs with hers so you couldn't move, I never figured out how she did it. Even up to the age of 23 she would jump on me and say 'play with me, Dad!'

I recall one day when she was around five years old I took her to the GPs because of some illness. Both Nicola's Mum and I were sitting in the crowded waiting room waiting to go in to see the doctor when she sneezed and announced to the waiting room that she had 'followed through'. As you can imagine the waiting room erupted with laughter, including me, though Nicola's mum wasn't impressed at what I had been teaching her!

Although she was a sociable child, she tended not to get involved in teams at school, and loved her schoolwork - that was one way we were different! In that respect she was more like her mother. Each evening she would finish her homework before she did anything else, and her school reports were always excellent. Every parents' evening was the same, with glowing reports about how well Nicola was doing.

She's beginning to sound like a swot, but Nicola was no bookworm. She was a pretty little girl who liked to look nice and loved to paint her nails. I remember one year she painted each nail with Christmas decorations on them, really neatly - her attention to detail was amazing. I could never have done anything like that.

In some ways she was a very conventional little girl, and her favourite toy when she was ten or eleven years old was Barbie. One year we went on holiday to Disney World in Florida, and in the Disney shop there they had every Barbie you could think of - there must have been 300 of them. She'd have bankrupted me buying them if she could have. By the time she grew out of Barbie she must have had about 20 of them including a purpose-built Barbie house with doors that opened up to expose the whole house with lights in each of the rooms. It even had a garage underneath for Barbie's car.

At times I would position Sam's action man on the toilet so Nicola would see it when she came home from school. 'Daaaad! What have you done *again*?' she would shout.

When Nicola was about ten years old she developed an interest in karate, which was a hobby I had been practising myself since 1983. By this time Sam would be about seven, and together they joined the karate club in Oldham which I was involved with and went on to run. In due course Nicola became a green belt. Her cousin Naomi and a friend all trained together and graded through the belt system together. We would train every Tuesday and Thursday, and on the way home through the village roads Sam would sit on my knee and steer while Nicola would change the gears, just for a few hundred yards, but all that stopped when they both rushed into the house to tell their Mum they had been driving!

We used to enjoy a lot of fun and games together and she always had a great sense of humour. She used to call me 'Dadzilla'.

In her teens she became very feminine and started paying great attention to her hair, make-up and nails. She hated the fact she had to wear glasses and a brace for a short period and said that as soon as she could she would be having laser eye surgery. When she eventually did have it she needed to have special treatment due to her complications with her eyes. She had huge eyes.

Nicola was always very sensible about boyfriends, but she certainly had some admirers. I remember one young lad coming calling one evening. Sam told me who he was, telling me 'he's a freak, Dad'. I had just returned home from work and was still in my uniform, so jokingly I yanked the door open and said 'what do you want?' in my most intimidating voice. The poor lad had quite a shock, but I must confess that Sam and I did have a laugh. Nicola was furious. 'Get out of my way, you're showing me up!' she snapped.

She was fifteen or sixteen when she had her first steady boyfriend. My mum called him 'Ronaldo' because he looked a bit like the footballer. But she was never one to get in too far with boys and she was quite clear that she was in no hurry to get married and didn't want kids, or certainly not yet. 'They ruin your life, ruin your finances, ruin your body,' she would say, though she was certainly fond of her friends' children and would play with them for hours.

Nicola loved amusement parks like Alton Towers. We spent most of our family holidays in the sun - usually Spain, the Greek islands or Florida - or sometimes we'd just drive over to Wales. She was a real sun goddess, and she used to turn a lovely dark golden brown. But even on the beach she was always very responsible and she would plaster herself with sun cream. In fact a lot the time it felt as if she was the adult in our relationship. 'Dad, grow up!' she would say. Or, 'Behave yourself!'

She was very public-spirited even as a young girl, and I remember her telling me I had to go and fix the windows for an elderly neighbour of ours. She would often volunteer me to help people out if she couldn't help them herself. I remember one time her class were going swimming and they needed help. She said she had looked at our diary and seen that I had a rest day, so she had told the head teacher I could do it. I expected to look after one boy, but as I got on the bus I was informed I was looking after 26 of them because there was no male teacher and Nicola had said it would be ok!

At the end of her time at Diggle primary school there was a school trip organised taking the children on an organised cycle trail. Again Nicola checked my schedule and duly volunteered me, saying, 'It's OK because my dad can ride a bike'. I ended up cycling 26 miles that day along with several other 'volunteered' parents. I struggled to walk for a week afterwards. Thanks again Nicola!

From the age of fifteen she worked in a pub, the Bull's Head Tapas Bar in Delph, waiting at tables to earn some spending money. A couple of years later I had separated from Nicola's mum and was with my new partner Nat, now my wife. I made the extra effort to spend time with Nicola and one evening she booked my partner and me into the tapas bar. She ordered for us and chose one of everything from the menu. Her explanation was that she got commission on sales!

She also worked at a local shoe shop in Oldham with a good friend from school, Georgie. She was very keen on making a bit of money and starting to save. Although she was generally sensible with her earnings in most respects, she did spend a fortune on make-up. She would dye her hair a different colour every six weeks. Its natural colour was golden brown, but you'd be hard pushed to tell!

I felt Nicola had managed to inherit the best of both of us. She had my sense of humour and my drive and stubbornness, but she also had her mother's ability to manage things and focus on detail. She was always scrupulously fair and honest. I remember she once told me her mother had given her £100 towards an expensive new coat she wanted and she asked me if I would match it. I always knew she wasn't playing games with us to get what she wanted, she was determined that it would be fair.

Unfortunately our marriage was going wrong by now and when Nicola was seventeen or eighteen, her mother and I separated. We had been together for some time and we both formed new relationships. Naturally Nicola stayed in the family home with her mother and Sam, but there was no question of us drifting apart as so many parents and kids do when the parents split up.

She was very mature about the break-up and very supportive to both of us and to her young brother. 'You're only 42 and you're not a bad-looking dad,' she said, even offering to take me speed-dating if I wanted. She just wanted us both to be happy.

Within a couple of weeks of me moving out, Nicola was in touch to say she wanted to meet my new partner, Natalie. We arranged to meet for lunch, and there was no hanging back, no suspicion - as soon as Nat walked in Nicola jumped up and gave her a hug and a kiss. 'You're making my dad happy' she told her. They got on great from the first. Nat is 17 years younger than me, so roughly nine years older than Nicola, and they had plenty of things in common, like make-up and hair products!

Natalie:
At first when Nicola knew about me and her dad she didn't want anything to do with me, but a few weeks later when we were away on a break she rang him on his mobile and said she wanted to meet me. Bryn and I arranged to meet her in a pub, and the minute Nicola walked in we just clicked. She gave me a friendly kiss and we got chatting immediately. It was easy from the first moment. It helped that there wasn't that much between us in age - I was only 26 and she was 18. There was never any time when it was awkward - we were instantly at ease together.

Nick and I didn't share all that much by way of interests, but we had very similar personalities - same sense of humour, same approach to life. We just 'got' each other. A few weeks later she came down to see me one day - me, not Bryn - and I remember we just sat on the sofa and talked, and it was like we'd known each other for ages. I would have made an effort to make it work between us anyway of course because of Bryn, but I never had to. We were close almost immediately. It's not something that you can make happen. Within a very short time it was just as if we were family. We used to make fun of Bryn, pulling his leg about his age and pretending that we'd put him in a care home.

The first time she came to tea at our house, she started groaning in pain. Sam said, 'You've poisoned her!' but she wasn't joking - it was appendicitis. She had to have an operation, so she had a flower tattoo put over it to hide the scar. I swore I'd never have a tattoo, so she would be laughing now that I have had her collar number tattooed on my wrist in her memory.

I can't help thinking how much Nick and I have lost together. She was so young. We could have been close friends for 50 years or more.

In 2009 Nat and I married. Nicola was our bridesmaid and Sam was an usher, although he created more noise than anyone else later. I remember Nicola walking into the hotel reception room where the wedding ceremony was taking place. As she walked in front of Nat wearing her off-the-shoulder bridesmaid's dress I noticed the two sea horses tattooed on her shoulders for the first time, and muttered to her, 'what the hell are they?', to which she replied 'Get over yourself Dad'. Even when I said 'That's it, your grounded,' she came back with 'Yeah right, in your dreams'.

As Nicola grew up she matured into a very strong-minded young woman who always knew what she wanted and where she was going. What you saw was what you got with her, and she knew how to get the better of me from an early age. I recall one day when she came home from school we were disagreeing about something and she came back with, 'It's not a rhetorical question!' I had to go and look up 'rhetorical' in the dictionary. She was only 13 then.

When she was about 21 Nicola started going out with her first serious boyfriend, Gareth, or 'Gaz-gaz' as she called him, who she'd met while working at the Bull's Head. I met him for the first time just before our wedding, and I remember saying at the wedding later, 'It will be you two next Nik'. 'No way' she said, 'I'm not wasting money on a wedding.' They were together for over three years and Nicola got him interested in policing. In fact he became a Special Constable with Greater Manchester Police.

By this time I was working at HMP Wakefield in West Yorkshire, a Category A prison housing the most dangerous prisoners in society. Ironic really that I have locked up some notorious prisoners who have themselves killed police officers. Little did I know that before long I would be looking at it from the other perspective.

Nicola always knew where she was going in life. Her grades from sixth form college were extremely good, and she excelled in both Law and Psychology. I tried to persuade her to study law at university and train as a solicitor, but she was more interested in psychology.

About this time we both read a book called *Good Guys Wear Black*, about the officers of the police rapid response firearms unit - not typical reading for a young woman, but it showed where her interests were going. She also read a book written by the retired pathologist at Oldham Hospital, and for a time she wanted to be a pathologist herself, but although she was tough she didn't like blood. However, her mind was made up - she wanted a career in either the armed forces or as a firearms officer in the Police.

On leaving Sixth Form College, she got a place to read social sciences and psychology at Huddersfield University. By then I was the Sex Offender Treatment Programme Manager at Wakefield Prison, managing treatment programmes for the inmates. I arranged for Nicola to visit the prison and look at the prison psychology department. She came in on the train so I could drive her home later. She chatted to the psychologists and asked all kinds of penetrating questions about the psychology of criminals and prisoners. I think she found it an interesting day, but on the way home in the car she told me it wasn't what she wanted to do as a career. "I don't want to be one of those!" she said.

It was then that she decided to apply to the police force. Although she hadn't yet finished her university course, she went ahead with an application and was accepted in 2008, when she was 19½. She didn't complete her degree course but instead started her police training a few months later in August 2009, when she was 20. That was when her adult life really began.

CHAPTER 2

On the beat

I was very proud of Nicola for making the decision to go into such a worthwhile career, and I knew from the start that she would make a brilliant copper. Despite what I'd seen in my own job, I never worried about her safety. Even though she was a slim girl, no more than about five foot six and nine stone, I could tell she had the ability to talk herself out of trouble.

I knew many police officers through the prison service, and I had spent two years with the police in a secondment role years before, so I felt she would be among friends and would be well looked after.

Nicola could be very determined, and if there was something she wanted to do she would really strive for it. For example, when she failed her driving test she analysed exactly what had gone wrong. She spent more time to study and practise, then took it again four weeks later and passed. She was always very focused.

Becoming a police officer means undertaking a range of assessments and tests to show that you have the necessary qualities. You have to be good at handling people, communicating, problem solving and working as part of a team. You also have to have the sort of personality that enables you to stay calm and focused in a crisis, or when you are being abused or even attacked. It's a challenging job, and it has some aspects in common with the prison service. The initial development programme takes two years, first working under supervision and later spending some of the time working on your own.

When Nicola first joined she spent several months at a little semi-rural police station, Mossley in Tameside Division. As it happened, one of the psychologists, Kelly, who I had worked with and Nicola had met on her visit to Wakefield Prison, was starting with Greater Manchester Police on the same day. They met up several times during training and were both involved in an incident where they were burned by CS gas during training.

I felt sure Nicola would do well, and she made an impression from the beginning. Everything she did, she did properly. Later, when I was talking to Nicola's sergeant, he said that where some officers would be satisfied with a one-page witness statement, she would write eight or nine pages. Every 'i' was dotted and every 't' was crossed. When he saw her first arrest file he asked, 'Who's helped you with this?' She was most indignant. 'No one's helped me,' she told him.

Police recruits learn partly on the job and partly at college. Nicola travelled to Police College in Manchester for a series of training modules. In total there were something like 38 weeks of college, mixed with time spent with experienced officers.

She soon started to talk to me in police lingo. 'We arrested an IC1 today Dad' she would say (a descriptive identification code), or 'we had a good shout today, thieves on' (meaning thieves on the premises). She would always drive everywhere as fast she could, just like me. In fact she picked up a speeding ticket one day when she was off duty, after shooting past a roadside camera in a safety van, and had to attend a speed awareness course. When she attended the course, she didn't tell them she was a police officer. The guy leading the course was talking about concentration and the fact that Nicola had not seen the roadside camera van, and she replied, jokingly of course, 'how could I see it while I was texting?'

In fact Nicola loved driving and was very good at it - she did the response driving course which allows them to use 'blues and twos'. She failed this at first but studied hard for the next four weeks and passed. When I was speaking to her instructor he said how Nicola had identified her mistakes and agreed where she had gone wrong, something he was unfamiliar with as usually officers who fail are not very responsive to feedback.

Nicola took her responsibilities as a police officer very seriously. Once when I started talking to about her safety and said how I would react if I saw her having trouble in the streets, I said I would come to her assistance and look after her. She said 'No Dad, it's my duty to protect you!' And she wasn't joking either.

We would meet up every couple of weeks and chat for an hour or two about what we'd both been doing at work. We both knew some of the same criminals, but obviously from a different perspective. She loved the job, although she wasn't so keen on the shifts and on working in cold weather.

I recall that during the winter of 2010, which was particularly cold and snowy for a long time, Nicola rang me at work on a Saturday morning and I mentioned that some of my officers had been out in the cold on the exercise yard for nearly a full hour. 'Don't tell me about being out in the cold for a poxy hour' she said, 'I was outside last night for four hours and the temperature gauge in the van said minus ten degrees'.

She was very popular with her colleagues, and they soon learned to respect her courage and determination. On one occasion they were chasing a young bag snatcher, who obviously thought no young girl was going to stop him getting away, but she barged him into a shop doorway and held onto him until a colleague assisted in his arrest before he knew what was happening. He was a big bloke and apparently he was quite shocked. On one occasion she had to crawl into a house through a dog-flap and another time when some officers were trying to get into some premises, she was literally thrown over a garden fence so she could open the gate and let the other officers in. She landed in dog muck and had to hose herself down back at the station, but she made a big joke of it all. In fact when she returned to the local station she placed her boot on the radiator to dry out, obviously without first having cleaned the dog mess from it. Apparently it smelled the station out.

The day she got involved in her first pub fight, the sergeant who was with her, Steve Miskell, told me he hadn't been sure she was going to be able to cope with the violence - there were chairs and bottles flying everywhere. But the expression on her face as she started dragging one of the victims to safety told him all he needed to know. He said later that she had 'the body of a lion cub and the heart of a lion'. After everything had calmed down he took Nicola to one side and said 'You shouldn't have gone in there'. Nicola was adamant she wasn't going to sit back and was determined to get involved, but he pointed out, 'It's only over twenty-ones allowed'. No amount of training can really prepare you for an encounter like that, and it demonstrated that Nicola was made of the right stuff.

Steve Miskell described her to the *Manchester*

Evening News as 'Friendly, full of life, always willing to give a helping hand, keen as mustard, as brave as they come, the little chatterbox who always kept everybody else awake.'

In a tribute later, her Chief Constable, Sir Peter Fahy, said: 'Despite her young years, she was incredibly mature. She showed herself highly capable in situations of disorder, brave when searching apparently unoccupied premises and going into the unknown, but on the other hand she showed great compassion to victims of crime. On one occasion she stopped her police van to rescue a mouse which was being fought over by two cats! In her dedication and professionalism in the way she carried out her duties, she showed that policing is not about muscle but about reason, restraint and intelligence. She had a promising career ahead of her, but was driven not by personal ambition but by service to the public in need. Nevertheless it is her warm smile and her gentleness that stand out from every picture of her.'

Nicola soon became the life and soul of the local station and was very popular with her colleagues. She would organise social events, including the station Christmas party. She was also great with members of the public, particularly anyone who was in trouble. When an elderly woman died, she went back to the house on her way home from work to see that the family were OK. She had also filled in the form very considerately. Instead of just putting everything down in formal, cold report language, she had written it out properly, for example opposite 'where did the death occur?' she put 'at Marjorie's home' instead of just the address. In fact the family wrote to Nicola's superintendent praising her for treating the woman with humanity, and he later sent Nicola a handwritten letter congratulating her on the way she'd handled the case. He told me he hadn't hand written a letter for years but felt that this time it was the right thing to do. She was very proud of that letter.

Once her first year and her 38 weeks' training were under her belt, she went on response to Hyde police station, the HQ of the Tameside division. After she'd been in the job two years Nicola was paired with an experienced officer who had been in the custody suite for a significant number of years. He was sceptical when he was paired up with her and was asking, 'What's a young girl like that going to show me after two years in the job?' However with Nicola's attention to detail and diligence she soon won him over and was full of praise for her afterwards. 'I was wrong' he said, 'she taught me lots of things.'

Nicola told me she had decided to take the sergeant's exam once she had done another year on response. It's a good plan to get the exam under your belt so that when the right promotion opportunity comes up you can apply for it. But she wouldn't have applied for promotion straight away on getting her exam - she wanted to make sure she was ready for it. With her qualities and her attitude, there was no doubt in anyone's mind that Nicola had what it took to progress in policing.

My daughter wanted to make a difference. And she has made a difference, though in cruel and dreadful circumstances. I am incredibly proud of her.

CHAPTER 3

A phone call from hell

Tuesday September 18 2012 started like any other normal day. I had woken at 6am and started off on my usual journey to work at Wakefield Prison where I was an Operational Manager, or Principal Officer as it was then known (this was an acting position and I was preparing for my forthcoming promotion interview). The day was slightly different from usual, as I had spent the morning in my office preparing for the interview. Usually I would have had the radio on in the office and possibly had the home page open on my PC, and no doubt the BBC news page would have also been open.

Following the interview at around 1pm I decided to go home for the remainder of the day and spend the day preparing for three further interviews I had secured at other prisons. After collecting my personal belongings from my locker I left work at half past one and was driving home along my normal route when at about 1.45 my mobile phone rang.

The number, which I didn't recognise, came up on my hands free system in my car. The caller asked if I was 'Bryndon' and introduced himself as a detective chief inspector from Greater Manchester Police and said he needed to talk to me. My first thought was that it was someone who Nicola had spoken about when she had paid a visit to the prison with a colleague while in training. They had asked to look at how we deal with prisoners suffering from a mental illness and one of her trainers had asked other police officers to do the same.

'Bryn, where are you?' he asked. I told him 'I'm on my way home and I know what it's regarding'.

'No it's not and I need to speak to you', he said. 'I'm outside your house.'

Immediately I knew something was wrong.

'What's the matter?' I asked.

He didn't answer the question. 'Where are you?' he asked. 'I'll come and get you.'

'Why, what's happened?'

'Just tell me where you are and I'll come and get you.'

He'd got me worried now, but I couldn't figure out what was wrong. I didn't think it could be anything to do with Nicola, because I had seen to her the night before and I thought she had told me she was off for five days. In fact, I later realised she had said she was *on* for five days.

'What's going on?' I asked him. 'Is it Nat, is it Sam? It can't be Nicola, she's off work.'

'No Bryn, she's not,' came the reply,

'What's happened?'

'I really need to speak to you,' he said again.

'What's wrong, has she been hurt?'

I was still driving at this stage and was becoming increasingly oblivious to my surroundings. I didn't know where I was or what speed I was travelling at, and I was unaware of other cars around me.

'Please tell me what's happened' I said, but he replied again, 'tell me where you are and I will come and get you'.

Then that horrible realisation came. You know how the rest of the conversation is going to go, you know what's coming next. It's like watching a film on TV that you know the end to, but however hard you try there is nothing you can do or say to change the outcome or the ending. You can't rewind, you can't turn it over, you can't switch it off, and no matter how hard you try you can't prevent what's coming next.

'Don't you dare tell me she's dead,' I said. I realised that if she had only been hurt he would have said something like, 'Don't worry, she's been injured but she'll be OK'.

'There's no easy way of saying this' he said. 'Tell me where you are and I'll come and get you.'

Not my Nicky, please not my little girl!

I finally managed to stop the car and sat there shaking with shock and unable to process what was happening. *It's not real - it can't be! Can it? I'm in a dream or a nightmare. I just need to wake up.*

Finally I managed to pull myself together enough to ring him back and tell him I was on my way. I told him I needed to speak to my wife, and he said, 'It's OK, there are officers with your wife'. He obviously meant my ex-wife of course - he didn't realise I was talking about Nat and that Nicola's mother was my ex. Not his fault, but he could have been better briefed.

Once I set off driving again I needed to ring Nat, who was at work at Risley Prison. When she answered the phone I managed to blurt out, 'Nat, Nicola's dead'. I didn't think about how she would manage to drive home across the M62.

The DCI was still wanting to come and get me, but there was no way I could just sit in the car waiting for him to turn up. You think of the most simple things, like 'I don't want to leave my car here and I'll need my car in the morning for work', stupid thoughts like that.

I put my foot down and drove as fast as I could for my home. I pass through several speed cameras on that route and I must have gone through them all at 70 mph. Funnily enough, I never got a speeding ticket.

When I got to my house, the DCI and a sergeant

from GMP were there. I recall opening my front door and collapsing on the stairs in the entrance, as numbness, shock, disbelief, everything rolled into one.

I asked what had happened, how and where. He told me that Nicola and a colleague had answered a 999 call and had been shot by a wanted criminal. I instantly knew who it was because of the extensive media coverage of this person (I refuse to even say his name in the same breath or sentence as Nicola).

I remember him asking if I knew where Sam was because they hadn't managed to get hold of him. I rang his mobile and Sam answered, 'what do you want Dad, I'm in the gym?' I repeated this to the DCI, and then I knew I had to tell my son that his big sister was dead. How do you do this? How do you tell your only son that someone who he loved with all his heart and looked up to and had grown up idolising had been so cruelly taken away in such horrific circumstances?

I plucked up the courage to continue talking and told him that a police officer would be coming to collect him.

'Why, what have I done?' came the reply.

I said 'Sam, I am so sorry but Nicola has been shot and killed.'

'No Dad don't say that, please don't say that!' It was almost like the conversation I had had with the DCI on the phone a short while earlier.

We then climbed into the police car to travel over to somewhere. I had no idea where I was going - he must have told me but my head was spinning and I couldn't process anything. On the way across the M62 over the Pennines I sat in the back of the police car feeling totally numb and detached from what was happening, as if I was 20 feet up in the air and looking down on it all. People we passed seemed to be staring at us in the police car, and I was thinking they all knew who I was and where I was going - ridiculous of course, though they may have heard on the news by then what had just happened a few miles away. I thought I could see the sympathy in their faces.

The sergeant was driving and the detective was sitting beside him and none of us knew what to say, so we were just talking drivel to try and fill the silence. I kept telling myself, I'm not going to believe this, not till I see her in the mortuary. I kept thinking that any minute she'd appear and say 'Hi Dad, you all right? What's all this fuss about?' and that there would be a call to say it had been a mistake and it wasn't really Nicola but someone else. I didn't care if it was someone else, just as long as it wasn't my little girl.

I recall the DCI talking on his phone saying 'We've got the father and taking him to…' I thought this was the name of a police building, not realising it was actually the name of the cul-de-sac where Nicola lived with her mum.

When we got to Nicola's home in Diggle I was met by a superintendent and two people who I was later told were the two family liaison officers, as well as various other officers. There seemed to be about 20 people in there, including my ex-wife's partner, who I've known for over 40 years. He was in shock too. Everyone was.

Sam had been collected by this time and was taken to his mum's. He was living with my mum, his Nan, who was 73 then. She spoils him rotten. He had got out of the shower because he had come straight from the gym and was crying and asking me, 'What the fuck Dad? What the fuck?'

They started to explain to me what had happened. It seemed there had been a shooting and that Nicola and a colleague, PC Fiona Bone, had responded to a call to go to a house in Hattersley, about three miles east of Hyde. Unknown to them, it was Dale Cregan who had made the call under a false name, and he was lying in wait. He had watched the van arrive, watched them get out, and as they had walked down the short pathway, he had opened the door and fired a number of shots at them. Apparently Fiona had died at the scene and Nicola had died by the time they had got her to hospital. The rest of the details were very sketchy and had not quite filtered through to us.

One of the FLOs asked me if we needed to inform anyone else, because the press were banging on the door wanting names and pictures. I had this vision of lots of men wearing hats with old cameras knocking at the door outside, like the typical scene you would see from an old film. I immediately thought of my mum, Nicola's Nan, and tried to ring her, but her phone was switched off, so I knew she must be in the bingo hall. When two police officers finally reached her she went through all the names of people who might have been hurt. She never thought of Nicola. She collapsed when the officer told her what had happened.

When the police first came to break the news to Sue, Nicola's mum, her first reaction had been to say that they should get hold of me, because Nicola and I had the same blood group, Group O Rhesus negative. She had told them where I lived, my mobile number and where I worked. This was around 11.30, but it was to be over two hours before I was contacted, and by this time it was confirmed that Nicola was gone.

Life would never be the same again, for any of us.

★ ★ ★

Nicola's and Fiona's colleagues on Tameside Division first heard the news while they were holding their weekly team leadership meeting with Chief Superintendent Nick Adderley. The team were just sharing good news about improved performance across the division when the door burst open and a detective sergeant told them, 'You'd better come out, something's happening in Mottram'. Nick and his senior team got on the police radio within seconds and established that a shooting had been reported and that PCs Bone and Hughes could not be contacted.

Nick Adderley described events as follows:

'While this was going on there were messages coming through that at the same time Cregan had just confessed to killing two police officers. At that point my blood ran cold. I rang the duty inspector, and it was obvious that Fiona was dead and they were still working on Nicola. It wouldn't have made any difference who had attended. The paramedics did a fantastic job, but they were not survivable injuries.

'It was like an out-of-body experience. I had held a senior position in the armed forces and I had been in conflict situations, but this was like nothing else, because the rules of engagement were completely different. Two unarmed officers, young women in the prime of their lives, had gone to a routine call and been slaughtered.

'You go over and over in your mind all the planning you did and question whether you would have done anything differently. You just want to somehow make it right, and you can't.'

A statement was immediately made announcing that an officer had died and another had been critically injured, and that Cregan had given himself up at Hyde Police Station and been arrested. Chief Superintendent Adderley arranged for an officer on the Isle of Man to deliver the dreadful news to Fiona's parents there. By the time that had been arranged, the news had come through that Nicola too had been certified dead.

* * *

Over the hours that followed, the terrible details emerged of the unbelievable, unspeakable events of that morning. Nicola had been on response duty that morning, based at Hyde as usual, with her friend and colleague Fiona Bone. Fiona was the more experienced officer, and nine years older than Nicola at 32. She was making plans to get hitched to her female partner in a civil partnership ceremony, and all the talk between the girls was of the arrangements for this. Nicola often talked about Fiona, and it was obvious they were great friends and made an excellent team.

Response simply means going out in response to any 'shouts' - anything from a road accident to a domestic dispute. They started their shift at 7 am sharp, the only double-crewed team that day, and were due to finish at lunchtime. They had booked out Tasers and CS gas canisters, as was routine during Operation Dakar, as the hunt for Cregan was known. When any call came in that required police attendance, Fiona and Nicola would jump into their VW Transporter and head for the scene, Nicola driving, as she had the necessary driver training.

One of their first jobs, at about half past nine, was to take a woman to the central lockup in Newton Heath, Manchester, for interview. Ironically enough, as it happened, the reason the police were talking to this woman was that she was involved in the Cregan case.

At 10.20, Nicola and Fiona were asked to attend a dispute at the Job Centre in Hyde, where one of the staff had phoned the police to say that a man was refusing to leave and becoming violent. Nicola and Fiona headed straight to the Job Centre, but the man obviously thought better of getting involved with the police and before they got there they had another call to say that he had left, so there was no further police action required. They could have continued to the Job Centre to make sure all was OK, but there didn't seem much point, so they swung the van around and headed back to base. If they had carried on to the Job Centre, what followed on their next call would never have happened - or rather, it would have happened to a different response team.

Just before the Job Centre call came in, the police had taken another emergency call. The man on the phone gave his location as 30 Abbey Gardens, Mottram in Longdendale.

'Someone's just thrown a big concrete slab through me back window and run off' he told the officer who took the call.

'Do you know why they did it?'

'Ain't got a clue... I was upstairs and looked out the window and seen one boy runnin' off... about my size, about five foot nine.' The man gave his name as Adam Gartree.

'I'll get an officer up there' the operator told him.

'How long will it take, d'you know, roughly?'

'Because it's just happened it's gone in under priorities, so that's within the hour, certainly... we'll try and get there as soon as.'

'Thanks very much. I'll be waiting.'

It would have been the turn of another officer at Hyde to respond to this call, but he had only just got back from another job and was still doing his paperwork for that, so when Nicola and Fiona got to the station, having aborted the Job Centre call, they offered to respond in his place. They left the police station at 10.41 and headed for Mottram.

As they drove they contacted the comms and asked if there was any intelligence history on the address they were heading for. This was not a normal request, but this was not a normal day, so they were being careful. That morning, all the officers had been briefed about the hunt for Dale Cregan. But it seemed there was nothing to worry about - they were told that nothing unusual showed up for 30 Abbey Gardens.

The VW Transporter made normal progress, as this was a priority call but not an emergency, though the record shows that at one stage Nicola switched the blue lights on for 46 seconds - no one knows why and we never will know. Perhaps they pulled someone over for some reason. The GPS tracker on the van shows that they turned into Abbey Gardens at 10.52, pulled the van into the parking bay at the end of the cul de sac, climbed out of the van and locked it. Then they stepped over the low wall around the parking area, crossed the pavement, pushed open the garden gate of no. 30 and took the few steps up to the door.

As they approached the door it opened, to reveal Dale Cregan. His picture had been posted widely because of the manhunt, so it's likely that Nicola or Fiona, or both of them, would have recognised him and realised immediately that they had walked into a trap and were suddenly and without warning in very serious trouble.

Cregan gave them no time to react, and as far as we know, little or nothing was said. He simply raised his automatic Glock pistol and started firing. Neither of the women had time to press the alarm button on her police radio. Fiona just had time to pull out her Taser (the monitoring signals show that the Taser was fired just 18 seconds after the engine of the van had been switched off) but the barbs fired from it struck the ground; she must have been put out of action immediately.

Nicola and Fiona had some protection from the first shots, which were fired at their chests, because they were wearing body armour, but as Nicola turned she was struck by a bullet in her lower back, which severed her spine. Once the officers were down, Cregan continued firing bullets into them until he had emptied the gun, which had an extended magazine, of all 32 rounds. Fiona suffered between five and eight gunshot wounds, one of them in the heart.

Having emptied the gun, Cregan threw it to the ground and pulled the pin from a hand grenade he had been saving up for this moment, a Yugoslavian-made anti-personnel fragmentation grenade, its outer casing packed with 3000 metal ball bearings. He now pulled the pin and threw it at Nicola's motionless form, where it exploded. Leaving the two officers lying on the ground, he grabbed the keys to a blue BMW belonging to the occupants of the house and raced off in it.

The radio transmission record indicates that Fiona's radio was put out of action by a bullet no later than 10:53:40, barely a minute after Nicola had switched the van's engine off, and probably before that.

By 10.56, the police had begun receiving 999 calls from the residents of Abbey Gardens, plus one from a horrified window cleaner who was working next door to the house. Police radios are fitted with a GPS tracking device, pinpointing the location of the radio at any given time. The radios are also fitted with an emergency button which, when pressed, sends an audible alarm to the control room, and to every other radio on that channel. Sadly the telemetry and data obtained from the radios showed that both officers had been motionless for some time and had not had the opportunity to press their emergency buttons, such was the speed and ferocity of the attack. It was obvious that something terrible had happened.

Upstairs, the occupants of the house, a young couple by the names of Alan Whitwell and Lisa McIntosh, had effectively been held hostage by Cregan since the previous day and knew he must be planning something evil. Whitwell looked down from the front window and saw the carnage. He waited until Cregan had safely driven off before he too dialled 999.

A neighbour who heard the shots was the first outsider on the scene. When he rushed out to see what the noise was, he found the two women police officers lying terribly injured in front of the house, Fiona in front of the window to the side of the door, Nicola by the gate. While Fiona was motionless, it appeared that Nicola was still breathing.

The first police officers on the scene were PC Andy Summerscales and PC Donna Jones. PC Summerscales had seen Nicola fit and well less than four hours earlier, when they had both been among the officers receiving the morning briefing at Hyde Police Station. PC Donna Jones was a personal friend of Fiona's. What they found when they arrived in Abbey Gardens changed both officers' lives for ever.

Nicola was lying on the front path, while Fiona was slumped under the window to one side of the door. It looked as if she had made some attempt to avoid the bullets. The officers quickly established that Fiona was beyond help and Nicola, although she still had a faint pulse, had suffered injuries which were not survivable.

The officers were very quickly joined by a paramedic, Paul Ferguson, who arrived in a fast response vehicle. He confirmed that Nicola still had a pulse and with PC Jones' help he tried to keep her breathing and then attempted cardiopulmonary resuscitation (CPR). A second paramedic, Carl Hough, intubated Nicola in the ambulance, as her airways were blocked. She arrived at Tameside Hospital at 11.30, but after extensive attempts by the team there it was clear that nothing could be done for her and she was pronounced dead at 11.38. Fiona was pronounced dead at the scene.

By now the police had arrived at Abbey Gardens in force, and within a very short time the road had been cordoned off. A massive investigation would now begin, but no one had any doubt who had committed the crime.

Because of the manhunt that was going on, there was an instruction out for all paramedics to report to a motorway staging post before proceeding to any call, but the two who attended decided not to waste a second - they drove straight to the scene as fast as they could. I believe those paramedics should have got commendations, even though strictly speaking they broke the rules. All they knew was that two police officers had been shot - they had no way of knowing whether or not the killer was still on the scene. They took a chance in the hope of saving their friends and colleagues, but as it turned out that was impossible.

It was just unfortunate that despite the might of the police exercise and the determination of every officer to hunt Cregan down, there had been no breakthrough, no clues to where he was. He had not been spotted at any stage since his disappearance, nor did the address he chose for his terrible crime have any connections which might have led to the police associating it with their investigation. There was simply nothing to warn the authorities what Cregan was up to until it was too late.

The official review of the case* concluded: '[Nicola and Fiona] were the innocent targets of a wanted criminal intent on murder who literally ensnared them in a carefully-laid ambush that he executed in the most callous and cold-blooded way. Given Cregan's intent and firepower, once they were out of their vehicle and outside the address, there was no realistic prospect of a different outcome... Neither of the officers could possibly have anticipated the malevolence that awaited them.'

* *Greater Manchester Police Health and Safety Review of the circumstances leading to the deaths of PC Nicola Hughes and PC Fiona Bone, quoted by permission*

* * *

CCTV cameras along the route soon showed the blue 3-series BMW driving back along the exact route Nicola and Fiona had taken from Hyde to Mottram, on to the M67 and into Hyde. It was a carbon copy of their journey in reverse, because Cregan's destination was the police station they had left less than half an hour before. He skidded sideways into the car park, pushed open the door and swaggered into the front office, dressed in a grey top, blue shorts and trainers. The officer whose turn it had been to attend the fake call to Mottram happened to see him arrive and started to tick him off for his reckless driving. But then, with his mobile phone under his chin as he talked to his girlfriend, Cregan told him 'I've just done two coppers'. He stretched out his wrists across the counter to be handcuffed, and the officer realised that this was the man they had been hunting all that summer.

Cregan told the officer he had dropped the gun at the scene. He went on, 'You were hounding my family so I took it out on yous [you plural]'.

The officer acted quickly and efficiently, vaulting the counter to make sure of a safe arrest. Within moments, a cold-blooded murderer was under lock and key for good (you can see a compilation on YouTube of the CCTV footage of his arrival at the police station and arrest).

The nearest Cregan came to expressing any words of regret, then or at any other time, was when he said he would rather his victims had been men.

Why did Cregan immediately hand himself in? Simply because he was afraid of a violent encounter with the law. He had jettisoned the gun and the grenades because he knew that if he was intercepted on the way to the police station, he would be facing armed police, and would very likely end up facing an end as brutal and bloody as the one he had just dished out to those two innocent officers. To quote Nick Adderley: 'Dale Cregan is a coward. If you look at his miserable criminal career, he's been a coward in everything he's ever engaged with. He claimed to have handed himself in because we couldn't catch him. The reality is that he is a coward who feared for his own safety and his own life, and that's why he handed himself in. That's also why he changed his plea later, because he was hoping that by finally admitting the murders he would get a more lenient sentence.'

★ ★ ★

I've dealt with quite a few difficult situations during my career in the Prison Service. Because of the very nature of the day-to-day work in a prison you become somewhat desensitised to the type of things that others would find difficult, stressful or abhorrent. Usually I'm the kind of person who can pull himself together without too much trouble, but this was totally different. Losing a child is the worst thing that can happen to you, particularly if it's without rhyme or reason and completely out of the blue, and I was really struggling. I didn't know the details at first and I imagined she'd just been unlucky and stopped a bullet. I thought that some people can be shot and stabbed half a dozen times and are still alive, why did she die after being shot once?

What I didn't realise at that stage just what he had done to Nicola and Fiona.

The rest of the day was a blur, people coming and going, phone calls, requests for information, who have we not told? So many people had to be told, and unfortunately we didn't manage to tell everyone before they saw the breaking news story.

That evening we met with the Assistant Chief Constable, Dawn Copley, and Nicola's Divisional Commander, Nick Adderley. You could tell how much they cared and how much they felt for us as a family, lasting friendships through such dreadful times.

I was desperate to see Nicola that day but was told that this wouldn't be possible because of what was happening in terms of the investigation process, which obviously meant the post mortem. It's a strange thought knowing that your own daughter is going through that and they are alone. You know at this stage there is nothing you could do for them, but it is really harrowing accepting that.

The following day we had various meetings with numerous people and were waiting patiently to go to see Nicola. My wife and I were in Manchester for a meeting with the Home Secretary when we received a phone call to say we could go and see Nicola, who had been taken to the new central mortuary in Oldham. There was no need for any formal identification because of the circumstances.

By the time we arrived it was around 8 pm. We pulled into the hospital car park, the same hospital car park I had pulled into on the night Nicola was born just 23 years and 11 months before, only this time I wouldn't be leaving it feeling the same as I had all those years ago.

The only two people allowed to see Nicola at this stage were myself and Nicola's mum. I'm not sure whose rules these are or why this was, but it was something that I resented and still do to this day. The only person I could turn to for comfort and support was my wife Nat, and she wasn't allowed to be there by my side. I was even told that she would have to wait in the car park outside. Imagine the thought of my wife sitting alone in the car in the car park of the hospital mortuary knowing what I was walking into. Needless to say she didn't, and she waited in the waiting room of the mortuary.

As she walked into the entrance, she collapsed in tears on the floor. It was Nicola's mum who insisted that the police officers should allow her into the waiting room.

It was explained to us how Nicola looked and what visible injuries she had. Nicola had had a little cuddly toy called George since she was born. I'm not even sure what George was any longer because he had been through the wash that many times. His eyes had worn off and there wasn't much pattern left on him, but he was still George and he needed to be with Nicola, so we took him with us.

At first it was thought that we would only be able to see her through the glass, but before we went into the room we were told that we would be allowed in and that Sue would be able to put George in Nicola's arms.

Finally I found myself looking at my beloved daughter. It just didn't seem real. They say you don't believe that someone is really dead until you see them, but even when I saw her I still didn't really believe it. She was lying there in a paper gown, with a big bandage round her head, and it looked as if she was asleep. She looked so small and tiny.

Walking in through that door was the hardest thing I have ever done and it was probably the hardest thing any parents would ever have to do, seeing your daughter, your child who you had cared for and loved all their life, lying there motionless, lifeless and so vulnerable.

Why, why, why? This can't be true, I kept thinking, it can't be! Again it was as if I was taking part in a horror movie and that it would end any minute and Nicola would jump out laughing in that way she had. Such a mockingly evil laugh she did, '*mmmwwwahhhh!*'

I didn't want to leave her, alone in the mortuary that night. 'She will be frightened,' I told myself.

We drove home along the M62 across the Pennines. Nat was driving and I was sitting there in the passenger seat, numb with grief and shock. I'm not sure if it's right or good practice to be expected to drive yourself home after an experience like that, but that's what we had to do.

Nat was aware that it was upsetting for me to be asked questions, but she wanted to know how Nicola was, a strange concept, but you find yourself thinking, I hope she was all right.

The following day again we prepared ourselves to take Sam and my mum to the mortuary, and this time we were able to be calmer and a little more at peace. Nicola had once teased her brother by saying he looked like a canary in his bright yellow tracksuit. He looked down at his big sister lying there and said, 'If you think I looked like a canary you look like a nun', and then he just started crying. He had called me that morning to say how he was scared to go and see Nicola and he didn't know what to do. I said 'Sam, I don't know what to do either'.

The whole community, the whole country, was in a state of total shock. Inspector Ian Hanson, the chairman of the Greater Manchester branch of the Police Federation, said 'This was a cold-blooded murder, the slaughter of the innocent. It's a dark day for policing and it's a dark day for society'.

* * *

On the Friday the Prime Minister himself came up to see us. Of course the shooting was massive news by then and there was little else in the headlines, but this meeting was held in private, thank goodness. There were about a dozen people gathered in the room with David Cameron.

That was also the day we met Fiona's parents, June and Paul Bone. Obviously we were and are united in grief, we understand what they are going through, and they understand what we are going through. So much in common, for all the wrong reasons.

The same day we had to go and see the investigating officer so that he could describe to us exactly what had happened to Nicola. He explained that the rules said that only Mum and Dad could listen to all this and that Nat and Sue's partner Mike could not be present. The 'rule book' that was quoted at the mortuary was being quoted again. I would like to see it some day and look for the part where it says 'treat the parent or step-parent like they don't matter'.

Obviously we knew that the cause of death had been multiple gunshot wounds. The first shot had hit Nicola in the chest and her body armour had stopped the bullet. This obviously knocked her down, and as she got to her feet while turning to get away the second shot went under the armour and into her spine, paralysing her immediately.

Nicola was right in the line of fire. Fiona managed to get to one side and draw her Taser before he fired again and killed her outright. We think Nicola tried to turn over to get up, but he blasted her with more bullets in the head and body. And then before he got into the car, in a final degrading act of callousness he threw the grenade towards them, with Nicola bearing the brunt of it.

We didn't realise how many times Nicola had been shot or how bad her injuries were until we spoke to the investigating officer. It was unspeakably brutal. The only consolation is that with the time frame of around 13 seconds (based on the GPS vehicle tracking, the short walk to the property and Fiona's Taser firing), she would have had very little time to realise what was happening or to suffer.

CHAPTER 4

Trail of hate

Dale Cregan was the lowest of the low, notorious in Manchester's gangland and particularly in his native Droylsden in east Manchester for his lawless exploits. He had turned to a life of crime almost as soon as he could walk, and was making a living from it in his teens. By the time he reached his twenties he was making enough money from drug dealing to drive expensive cars and take exotic holidays. Somewhere along the way he lost an eye, which made his appearance all the more intimidating.

Cregan had a number of almost equally violent sidekicks who helped him with his sordid exploits. Their principal enemies and rivals in the Manchester area were the Shorts, a well-known family of criminals who were based in Clayton, a few miles out of the city to the north east. David Short, the head of the family, had convictions for assault, grievous bodily harm, drug dealing and threatening witnesses, among others. In 2006 he was jailed for six years for possession of a firearm with intent to cause fear. Two years before that, he had been formally warned by the police that he had made so many violent enemies that his life was in danger.

Short's son Mark, an amateur boxer, followed his father into a life of crime. In 2008 he was sent down for five years for robbery and GBH.

Following a violent clash in a pub between David Short's long-term girlfriend and a woman from another gangland family, the Atkinsons, a long-running family feud between the Shorts and the Atkinsons was rekindled. One of those who hated the Shorts as much as the Atkinsons did was Dale Cregan. The Shorts had upset Cregan in the past by invading his 'manor' in Droylsden, and when he heard about the spat in the pub, he decided to take revenge on the Atkinsons' behalf. On a hot summer's night in 2012, backed by a group of accomplices to mind his back and drive a getaway car, Cregan walked into the Cotton Tree pub in Droylsden and blasted away with a pistol. He fired seven rounds, shooting Mark Short dead as he played pool in the back bar and injuring three of the men who were with him. David Short escaped only because by chance he had gone to the gents' at that moment. Hard man as he was, he was devastated when he saw the bloodied body of his son.

Greater Manchester Police had a pretty good idea who the killer was, but over the weeks that followed they had trouble piecing together the evidence they needed to arrest him. Cregan was free to take expensive overseas holidays, and although he was arrested in June he and his accomplices were released on bail pending further enquiries. Then on August 10 2012, having evaded the law by the skin of his teeth, Cregan, aiming to reduce the chance of a revenge attack against him by the Short family, finished the job he had started in the Cotton Tree by killing David Short at his home. He had tried lying in wait for him in the cemetery where Short would visit his son's grave several times a day, but kept turning up at the wrong time. Instead, on August 10th, he and an accomplice, Anthony Wilkinson, went to Short's home in Woodhouses, where they found Short out by his car. After chasing him into the garden and firing at least ten bullets from two semi-automatic handguns into him, Cregan made sure Short was dead by blasting him with a hand grenade as he lay on the ground.

Not satisfied with this, Cregan, Wilkinson and another accomplice, Jermaine Ward, went to the home of a man called Hark, with whom Cregan had a score to settle for some reason. Hark and his friends had a lucky escape - Cregan's gun jammed, and when he tried to throw a grenade into the front room it bounced off the window frame and exploded outside.

Where did Cregan get his weapons from? His store of hand grenades - eventually the police found them in a drain - were of Yugoslavian manufacture and are thought to have been among many smuggled across by criminals in the aftermath of the Balkan wars in the 1990s. He admitted to owning some 10 illegal firearms, including a Glock 9mm automatic pistol, the one used in the murders in Abbey Gardens, and a .45 pistol which was also used in the killing of David Short.

The evidence Cregan and his mates left behind was enough this time to make sure of a conviction, and Cregan went on the run. He split from his two principal accomplices, Jermaine Ward and Anthony Wilkinson, and by the end of August both Ward and Wilkinson were in custody and giving valuable evidence to the police.

Now the full might of the law was on the trail of Dale Cregan, who had become the UK's no. 1 most wanted man, particularly given the access he had not just to guns but grenades. This would be the largest intelligence-gathering network ever conceived by a UK domestic police force where terrorism was not involved. Under the name Operation Dakar, a fully-staffed incident room was set up and every officer in the county was briefed to be on the lookout for Dale Cregan. Other police forces were alerted, and everyone up to the Home Secretary was kept in the loop. Up to 14 armed response vehicles at a time were deployed daily to undertake armed patrols. Ward and Wilkinson soon found themselves in custody, but Cregan remained elusive.

The focus of the search was naturally Manchester - no one knew that by now Cregan was actually holed up in a flat in Leeds. Those who were close to Cregan or his enemies were given 'threat to life' warnings by the police (David Short had received three), and by the end of the investigation more than 100 people had received 'TTL' warnings. A list of high-risk addresses was compiled, and if anything came up which was connected to one of them, special action was taken; for example, when a brother of Cregan reported a fight between his mother and sister, the address was flagged as a high-risk one and an armed response vehicle was deployed for the initial response - just in case.

Police carried out more than 60 armed raids on suspect properties around Manchester. Pressure was put on Cregan's friends and family to accept that the police wanted Cregan captured safely and that his best option was to surrender peacefully. A reward of £25,000 was offered for information leading to his arrest, and in the last week of August it was doubled to £50,000, an almost unprecedented sum. Unfortunately it seemed even this wasn't enough to persuade any of the criminal underworld who had useful information about Cregan to risk putting their lives on the line. Given that the manhunt was costing an estimated £150,000 a day and the eventual overtime bill came to over £1 million, there was a feeling - there still is - that the reward money was still nowhere near high enough.

Front-line officers like Nicola and Fiona were given extensive briefings on the situation and told how to react if there was an encounter with Cregan. The need for extra vigilance was stressed and advice was given not to approach him, and how to minimise the danger if any officer was faced with the prospect of guns or grenades being used against them.

Unsuspected and unobserved by anyone, Cregan was meanwhile planning a still more barbarous and shocking finale to his trail of destruction. In order to carry it out he returned to the Manchester area and picked a house at the end of Abbey Gardens, a cul de sac in Mottram in Longdendale. Number 30 was the home of Alan Whitwell, a young barber whom Cregan had patronised in the past. Whitwell was living there with his girlfriend, Lisa McIntosh, and her seven-year-old daughter. Cregan picked this house because it gave him an uninterrupted view along the road, perfect for the ambush he was planning. Mottram was not one of the areas estimated by the police as being at high risk in the Cregan manhunt, as it was thought more likely their quarry would surface in his regular 'manor' around Droylsden or Clayton.

Late on the evening of Monday September 17, Cregan knocked on the door of no. 30 and walked in. He then proceeded to effectively take the family hostage and keep them prisoners in their own home overnight.

'I was getting ready for bed when I heard a knock at

the door' Whitwell said in an interview. 'I recognised the man as Dale Cregan. He said, 'Do what I say and you won't get hurt'. I couldn't believe it. I didn't know what to do.'

Lisa McIntosh described how Cregan put a hand grenade on the mantelpiece and a gun on the sofa, and said she was terrified for her life and her daughter's. He proceeded to toy with his weapons and to have a drunken 'farewell party' for himself while the family huddled in fear upstairs.

It was understandable that Alan Whitworth and Lisa McIntosh were in fear of their lives, although it emerged later that they did have at least one opportunity to raise the alarm. At one stage Cregan took a bath alone upstairs, and the following morning, before the ambush was set, all three of the family were at one point out of the house together; Whitwell was instructed to go to work as normal, to avoid anyone's suspicions being aroused, and Lisa McIntosh took her daughter to school. After attending work for a short time, Whitwell, anxious about his family, made an excuse to return home. At this point Cregan, who was vain about his appearance despite having only one eye, then ordered him to give him a haircut and trim his beard.

Alan Whitwell explained: 'People might wonder why I didn't ring the police... I didn't know what time Lisa would get back to the house... I didn't want to risk ringing the police, because if Lisa was still in the house and there were armed police she'd be in big danger'.

Lisa said that when she left to take her daughter to school she was telling herself she should raise the alarm, but she was afraid of the consequences if Cregan found out, so she did not. Of course the couple had no idea what Cregan was planning, although they did know that he was already wanted for two murders and he had told them he had killed David Short.

Alan Whitwell had just returned from work shortly before 11 am when he looked downstairs to see Cregan walking towards the front door with the gun in his hand and muttering something about 'police'. Then the front door opened and immediately Whitwell heard a series of loud bangs. Cregan then came back inside and asked for the keys to Lisa McIntosh's BMW, which the terrified Whitwell gave to him. He then looked out of the window to see Cregan pull the pin from the grenade and throw it back towards the house. There was a massive bang. Leaving the inert forms of PC Nicola Hughes and PC Fiona Bone where they had fallen in front of the house, Cregan jumped into the BMW and raced off with a squeal of tyres.

'I didn't want to ring the police until I knew he'd gone,' Whitwell concluded in his press interview. His partner added, 'You've got to live with the guilt every day. If we'd made a different decision, would those officers still be alive today? It still haunts us on a daily basis.'

Apparently they were not the only ones who were too afraid of the consequences to report Cregan to the police. One man told the *Manchester Evening News* that he had seen him in a pub not long before the murders, but did not pick up the phone to the police out of fear, despite the £50,000 reward which had been offered. The police view, however, is that the main reason Cregan was not spotted and reported in time was simply that he was so careful not to be seen anywhere in the areas where he might be recognised.

Unfortunately Cregan also had an ally within the police force. In December 2014, former Greater Manchester police constable Katie Murray was jailed for two years nine months for misconduct in a public office. She had been passing information about the hunt for Dale Cregan to an ex-boyfriend, Jason Lloyd, who was one of Cregan's associates. Lloyd was growing cannabis on a large scale and had persuaded Murray to get information from the police computer to help him evade justice. As a result a raid failed to reveal any cannabis plants, which had been hidden, although when the police returned later they found plants to the value of £300,000.

Murray, who had been serving with the force for ten years, had also posted a picture of Nicola on Facebook within half an hour of the murders and three hours before even her father could be told of her death.

CHAPTER 5

Beyond belief

When the news broke that two young women police officers going about their duty had been so savagely murdered, all hell broke loose. It felt as if every journalist in Britain was trying to get a piece of the action. We had a police press liaison officer assigned to us to deal with enquiries and they did their best to keep control of the situation.

Most of the journalists behaved themselves professionally and kept to the limits requested by the police, but there were some who overstepped the mark. We kept being asked, 'How are you feeling?' (What sort of stupid question is that?) Or 'Is this the worst day of your life?' or 'Are those tears on your face? Have you been crying?' I know they have their job to do, but I found all this unacceptably callous and intrusive.

I was driving back from the mortuary on the Thursday morning when the hands-free phone went. It was a sports reporter from the local paper. He had my number because of Sam's involvement in karate tournaments, so when he introduced himself as being from the sports desk, I thought it was about karate. 'Is it a good time to talk?' he said. 'No sorry, I'm a bit busy' I said. 'I'd just like to say on behalf of the staff here how sorry we are' he said. 'Can I just get your comments on what's happened?'

I thought, you sneaky b******! For me, that really tarnished that newspaper's reputation. Obviously someone on the news desk had said, 'You've got his mobile number, he knows you, get in there and see if you can get a comment for us.'

Having seen Nicola at the mortuary on the Wednesday, I took my mother and son to see her on the Thursday evening. When we got back and pulled up in the parking area outside the place where my mum lives, the press were waiting for us. One reporter came up to the car, pulled the door open and spoke to my mother. 'Hello, are you Joy?' he said. She was a bit startled, but she said yes, she was Joy. 'I just want to ask you a few questions,' he went on. 'What are you thinking now about your granddaughter?' Mum had only just seen her lying there in the mortuary!

Sam had just pulled up beside us, and he went crazy with this bloke. 'Who the f***** hell are you?' he shouted. 'I'll ram your f***** newspaper up your arse!' He chased him to his car and was trying to pull the door open before I stopped him. Sam is six foot two and 16 stone, so this chap must have been shitting himself, or at least I hope he was. I managed to pull Sam away even though I was drained and not slept for 48 hours.

Later a national newspaper contacted the undertakers to try to find out where the grave was, presumably so that they could take a picture of the gravestone.

Nicola was very friendly with a cousin her own age, who was almost like a sister to her. One evening in the pub, she was drawn into conversation by a man she knew of, who wanted to ask questions all about Nicola and what had happened. What she didn't know was that the conversation would be used to make headlines the following day. She was devastated about that and felt she'd let Nicola down as well as us. We didn't blame her in any way of course. She had just been conned.

For days after it happened, my ex-wife's home was besieged by the press, and the police stationed an officer in a car at the end of the cul de sac to give her some protection. There were press photographers at the end of the road, trying to get pictures. There's a hill a quarter of a mile from the house and a few days later the police saw a group of four or five men on the top of it, with telephoto lenses trained on Sue's house. They even had a drone and were trying to take pictures with that. But most of the journalists were respectful and kept within the agreed limits.

The statement we prepared for the press immediately after it happened read: 'Our beautiful daughter left home yesterday morning to do the job she loved. Nicola was our only daughter and a beautiful child. She was always happy with life and she lived for her family. She had an infectious personality and a great sense of humour and was a very caring and loving girl. Nicola always wanted to make a difference and in doing so, she made such a big difference to everyone she knew. She cared about everyone, and especially her colleagues.

'Nicola was only 23 years old and she had the whole of her life in front of her. We cannot express how we feel today except to say that we have always been exceedingly proud of Nicola and always will be. She knew she was loved by us all, and we will all miss her dreadfully.'

More than 50,000 people, few of whom of course had known Nicola or Fiona, signed books of condolences for them. A police tribute written on a bouquet of flowers summed it up: 'You've kept your promises, you've served and protected. Gone but never forgotten. With love, from all at E Response, Stockport.'

Nick Adderley told how an elderly gentleman had come into the station at Ashton and handed in £5.25 in coins. He explained that it was the money he could spare from his pension that month, and he wanted the police to have it. Nick said, 'While you've got people like that out there in the community who want you, need you and value you, it doesn't matter how many Dale Cregans you've got out there, we'll go on doing what we do to the best of our ability.'

The police cordoned off Abbey Gardens and put steel barriers around the garden of number 30, as it remained a crime scene for several weeks. They were still gathering evidence and there were grenade fragments everywhere.

A week after it had happened, to the day and the hour, we were invited to go there for a vigil, and that was the first time I had seen the place where my daughter had died. It was pouring with rain. They drove us up to the house in a van with darkened windows. The press crowded round and tried to take pictures of us through the van windows. They told us that if we preferred to we could stay in the van, but Sam said 'No, we're getting out', so we did. They gave us umbrellas and we walked up to the scene, and every time we moved you could hear the cameras rat-tat-tatting away.

Nearly all of Tameside Division Police Officers walked from Hyde to Hattersley and back to 'finish their shift'. It was pouring with rain and as you can imagine there was lots of press interest. I was a bit taken aback to see that they had built a temporary stage next to the site to give the press a better view. It did make us feel as if we were on show. Sir Peter Fahy said: 'Clearly this is one of the darkest days in the history of Greater Manchester Police. A week ago today, the world was deprived of two wonderful human beings. The police service lost two of its rising stars and the community lost two dedicated servants.'

One of the local residents, community volunteer Elsie Dixon, paid tribute to Nicola and Fiona and said their deaths would not be in vain. She said Hattersley was a 'community in mourning,' adding: 'Those two girls are precious. We are a community that cares, not just for ourselves but for each other and for the people that serve our community. Our police officers are part of our community and those girls were special.

Sue and I planned the funeral together. I wouldn't say all this brought us closer exactly, as we were both settled down with new partners and had been for some years, but obviously as parents you share the memories of all the things that happened when your child was little.

You never expect to plan your child's funeral. Granted some people plan their own, but to plan a child's is heartbreaking and unreal. So many people wanted to attend, so many dignitaries and so many friends and family, some we hadn't seen for many many years.

The long drive from Diggle to Manchester Cathedral was so difficult, but in the same sense it was comforting to see so many people standing at the side of the road as we passed. Some people threw flowers and applauded, some were crying, including people who didn't know Nicola and had never met her but felt as if they too had lost someone. They had lost a part of decent normal society where people respected the police and respected a person's right to continue living and enjoying life without some piece of evil scum doing what he had done.

Walking into the cathedral and seeing so many people all gathered to say goodbye and to support us as a family was overwhelming and walking in behind Nicola left you feeling proud about the amount of love and respect normal decent people had for my daughter.

Nicola's funeral took place on Wednesday October 3rd, a couple of weeks before what would have been her twenty-fourth birthday, at Manchester Cathedral. The whole of Deansgate in central Manchester was lined with the blue uniforms of police officers. They weren't just local officers but men and women from all over the country - every police force sent someone, and messages of condolence came from all over the world, from France, Italy, Germany, America, Norway, Portugal and Croatia, to name a few. They were given wristbands printed with Nicola's and Fiona's badge numbers. Behind the officers were thousands of ordinary people who had gathered to pay their respects.

Nicola's coffin, draped with a wreath of white roses, her gloves and her police hat, was borne on a cortege led by six police horses and carried into the cathedral by six of her colleagues. There were no politicians present, as it was agreed that this was a day for the police 'family' and for people who knew Fiona and Nicola to come together to pay their respects. The service was filmed and displayed on a giant screen outside the cathedral. Nicola's colleagues gave a number of readings.

At the private service at the Crematorium I chose to carry Nicola in along with Sam, Gareth and our good friend Kenny. Nicola had been a bridesmaid at Ken and Linda's wedding some years before.

The main pallbearer, a sergeant, said they should do this duty because they had trained for it and would like to finish off the day. Obviously I insisted we join them, saying 'I have carried her for 23 years, I've never dropped her yet and don't intend doing so now'. I didn't reveal that I had actually dropped Nicola when was she was about six months old when I fell asleep while nursing her. I never forgave myself for that and have felt guilty ever since (I never told her Mum about it!)

Standing there with my daughter on my shoulders was so so hard, and how I managed to walk into the crematorium I will never know. I could feel Sam's hand holding tightly onto mine underneath Nicola, a heart-breaking feeling even now.

Nat: Watching Bryn and Sam pick up the coffin at the funeral was one of the hardest parts of it all. I knew what was in that coffin, because I had seen it with my own eyes. Watching my husband carry his daughter's coffin broke me.

The bearers at the cathedral were all police officers from

Nicola's relief but at the crematorium Bryn, Sam, Gareth and our good friend Kenny all stepped in to replace some of them.

★ ★ ★

In the month that followed Nicola's death, my filling station receipts show that I spent £812 on diesel, in an ordinary Volvo saloon. So you can imagine how much motoring I was doing, going to meetings, briefings, debriefings, interviews and so on, all connected with the case. I was allowed to stay away from work of course, though I didn't officially take leave. I couldn't possibly have done my job in the state I was in. I was constantly in meetings, out all day and getting home at seven or eight at night. Being so busy did help a little.

Much later we returned to Abbey Gardens in private with the family liaison officers, who had asked some of the neighbours to keep away to give us some privacy. I noticed that they had resurfaced the path where all the blood must have been and I could see that there was a new paving slab stone near the gate in the spot where I knew Nicola had died. That was a chilling moment. I saw the low wall at the front of the parking bay, and imagined how she and Fiona would have got out of the van and stepped over it. I wondered what they would have been talking about in those last seconds and what would have gone through their minds when they were confronted by this man.

As we stepped into the garden, a woman came out of her house several doors away and shouted at us for trespassing. The police officer quickly ushered her away and explained who we were, and she was visibly upset. Of course she wasn't to know, she was acting in our own interests.

★ ★ ★

People say about grief that you move on, there are seven stages and it's this and it's that, but trust me, it doesn't work like that. Sometimes I went through those stages all together and sometimes in the wrong order, and that leaves you feeling very confused. There were some very dark days, as there still are and always will be. The stage you never reach is getting over it. All you can do is learn to live with it. Some time later my Governor, Susan Howard, likened it to a wound on your arm. At first it's really raw and sore. Then over time it scabs over, but you can't help but pick at it, which causes pain at times. Eventually it scars over, but it's still visible. You know it's there, you know why it's there and why at times it itches or is painful. You can't forget it or leave it alone, and you will always have the scar.

I like to think of grief as the angry dog in the back garden. If you lock it out in the pouring rain and don't feed it but give it a kick every time you see it, sooner or later it will bite you. It will bite you when you least expect it to and probably every time it gets the chance.

But if you feed and exercise it, keep it on a lead and muzzle it, then it won't get the chance to bite you.

I felt a huge amount of anger towards the so-called human being who killed my daughter. I never dignify him by speaking his name, to myself or anyone else. He's just a number where he is now. I don't want to waste any negative energy on him. As someone told me, 'If you hate someone too much it's like taking poison yourself hoping that he's going to die, or holding hot coals - eventually you are the one who will be burned'.

Instead I prefer to think of him as the complete nonentity he is. He didn't have the courage to go out in a blaze of glory by challenging the police. All he said at one point was, 'I wish it had been men'. As if that makes any difference. As if men don't have partners or children or families.

He had the choice that day to hand himself in, the option of putting down his gun and his grenades and thinking about what pain and heartache he was about to cause, not only to the two police officers approaching the door but to their families, for the rest of their lives. Obviously he was fully aware of what he intended to do, choosing the location and watching the van pull up with two unarmed female officers. Even if he had attempted to flee the scene and threaten Nicola and Fiona with the gun he would have succeeded.

Why didn't he choose to ring 999 and say who he

was and where he was? Because he knew the consequences. He knew full well that an armed response vehicle would have attended, and he would in all probability have been shot himself. Otherwise why did he drop the gun in the street and drive as fast has he could to the police station, a place of safety for him where he knew he would be on CCTV and wouldn't be harmed or risk being stopped on route by an ARV? Because, as Nick Adderley points out, he's a coward.

One way I have tried to vent my anger was training at the karate club where Nicola and Sam had also trained. Several years ago we completed a challenge where we all completed a thousand push-ups. I have some video footage of Nicola taking part and that is really difficult to watch. I didn't realise until recently but I was struggling making the effort to return to the karate club until I thought about the video. Every time I walked into the hall and saw our junior members training it reminded me of Nicola. Strange little things like that affect you so much at times.

I went through a stage when I was really angry every single time I got into the car. I've always been an impatient driver and at that time I was even worse than usual. Nat said I was frightening her. But if she drove, I was the world's worst passenger.

One day I was standing in the queue at Tesco when the guy in front of me was given his change in coins, because the cashier had no five pound notes. He looked at his change and said 'what am I supposed to do with that?'

She replied, 'I'm very sorry sir, we don't have any five pound notes'.

'Well that's not very convenient' said this bloke. 'Can't you get a fiver from another till?'

I could feel the anger welling up inside me. I could feel myself wanting to lay him out with a punch. I think he must have asked for that five pound note about half a dozen times. At this stage both Nat and I said to him 'you need to get a f***** grip!' 'Well that's a bit cheeky!' he said, but he got the message.

I don't suppose I was getting more than about ten hours' sleep a week, and you can imagine the dreams I was having - Nicola laughing and chatting, Nicola in her uniform, Nicola putting on her make-up and painting her nail polish on, Nicola as a little girl, Nicola doing her homework, always Nicola. I went to see my GP. I explained everything and then he said 'so why can't you sleep?' I felt like tipping the desk over. It was as if he hadn't listened to a word I'd said. Now I realise he was just trying to make me explain exactly what happened when I was trying to sleep. Things have got better slowly, but I still only get about four hours a night.

You wouldn't believe how many sympathy cards we got in the weeks after Nicola died. We had ten or twelve big boxes of them. We had cards from Prince Charles,

David Cameron and the Director General of the prison service. One sympathiser sent a photograph of a double rainbow which he had taken over Hyde the day Nicola and Fiona had died.

There was a street artist who drew a picture of the Queen crying a thin blue line, somewhat like a postage stamp portrait, and a tattooist in London contacted Greater Manchester Police to ask if I would like the image tattooed on my back! Obviously I declined....

Occasionally there was a lighter side to it. When you arrive at a prison you have to pass through a metal detector, the way you do at an airport. If you set it off, you get searched. On a visit to Wakefield Prison I was met by one of my colleagues, a woman who had joined the service the year I was born. She stretched out her arms and I thought she was signalling to me to put my own arms out to be searched, but it wasn't that - she just wanted to give me a big hug.

Sometimes people close to me seemed more upset than I was, certainly those who had known Nicola. When I was walking through Wakefield town centre one day, I couldn't help noticing that people who recognised me were crossing the road and looking the other way, because they couldn't deal with it. One bloke walked up to me and put his hand on my shoulder, then started crying and walked off without saying a word.

Between the funeral and the beginning of the trial, which was set for early in 2013, I went back to work at the prison just to keep my mind off it all. I was setting up a department at the time, which gave me something useful to do without having to deal with prisoners. Not surprisingly, I sometimes nodded off at my desk.

We lived from day to day as one day rolled into another, without any forward planning. There were endless meetings and events.

I had to make a victim impact statement, which without a shadow of doubt was the hardest thing I've ever had to write. It was so difficult trying to put all my tangled thoughts and feelings into words. I had to write about her life and what I thought she would have gone on to do. My ex-wife and I did consider writing a joint impact statement, but we had been apart for seven years and each of us now had our own thoughts and memories, so we did them separately. I did write it with Natalie's help.

Fortunately these statements were not read out in court, only referred to. The police press liaison officer said the press had asked for copies of them, but that was refused.

Nicky as a little girl

Nicky with (not so) little brother Sam

Dressed nicely for the camera

With her proud father

Play acting as usual

Looks like she stepped in something…

Karate Summer Camp 2005

Karate Club Christmas Party

Christmas with Dad

Having fun with dad again

My pretty little girl

Nicky, Dad, Nat and Sam at our wedding

Daughter of the bridegroom

The bridesmaid

Nicola with Nat at our wedding

Proud officer of the law – the photo that was used across the media

20 Abbey Gardens (in the centre) (Google Earth)

Hyde Police Station (Google Earth)

Abbey Gardens, with the investigation still going on

The tributes pile up at the entrance to Abbey Gardens after the murders

Police officers pay their respects

Nicky's fellow officers united in grief

Speaking at the British Women in Policing (BAWP) Awards in 2014.
We now sponsor the Bravery Award each year.

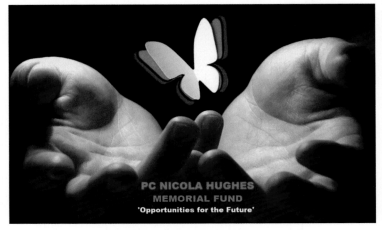

The logo for the PC Nicola Hughes Memorial Fund

At Leeds Metropolitan University, in training for the North Pole Marathon.
L-R Rob Stapleton, Dr Ben Jones, Dr Lauren Duckworth & me.

Training in sub-zero temperatures

On my way to the North Pole, with Rob Stapleton

Ready for the marathon

The athletes' 'village' at the Pole

Inside our tent

The Antonov cargo jet that flew us from Svalbard to the Pole

The huge Russian chopper that carried us to the magnetic North Pole

The run gets under way

There wasn't a lot at the North Pole apart from ourselves
and lots and lots of ice and snow

Being interviewed by the BBC

It helps to run with a companion

L-R Adam McClean from ITV, Rob Stapleton, me, Jim Cooke ITV

The sun never gets much higher than this at the Pole

Remembering Nicola at the magnetic North Pole

...and sometimes it's worth it

The ice got everywhere

A feeling of achievement

CHAPTER 6

Justice

The trial of Cregan and nine of his partners in crime for the murders of Nicola, Fiona and the two Shorts, plus the attempted murders of four other people, began on February 4 2013 at Preston Crown Court. It was billed as one of the biggest and potentially most expensive criminal trials there has ever been in the UK, and at one point there were rumours that it would have to be held at the Old Bailey. Imagine attending a five-month trial in London when you're living in the north-west.

Fortunately that didn't happen. Even so, it would have been impossibly gruelling for us to attend the whole trial, so we just went to the opening sessions and the summing up, closing statements and sentencing.

On the first day of the trial we were picked up in a police minibus, which was quite impressive. I had been involved in prisoner escort work of course, and I had spent six weeks at Preston Court for a trial, so I knew the routine and the court building very well, but it puts a very different perspective on it when you know who's inside the van and what they've done.

Although we were well looked after, it was quite overwhelming to arrive at the courthouse to be besieged by press photographers and film crews. You see all the flash guns popping away when scenes like this are shown on television, but the real thing is much more spectacular. The agreement was that we would let the press film our arrival on the understanding that they would leave us alone the rest of the time. We were told to keep our comments very brief and not to say where we worked, or talk about what sentences we wanted the criminals to get.

The security was huge at court, with dozens and dozens of armed and unarmed police officers in and around the court building. Entry into the court was as strict as airport security - they made you empty your pockets every time you went in. There was a whole team of prison officers looking after the accused. I had been through the same procedures so many times in my prison career but now that I was at the heart of a trial myself, it didn't seem real.

The court staff explained that the defendants' families had all been allocated two seats each in the public gallery. Fortunately all those seats weren't needed, as a lot of them were in prison or wanted by the police, so they weren't likely to be showing up in the courtroom!

In addition to the ten defendants and their families and legal teams - each defendant had his own QC, Junior Barrister and Solicitor - there were press seats in the court, along with additional press in an annexe upstairs, where the journalists were able to watch live pictures and sound from the court.

I felt there was nowhere near enough provision for the victims, as there could have been up to seven of us wanting to attend at the same time - myself, my wife, my son, Nicola's mother and her partner, my mother and Nicola's boyfriend Gaz. I feel that the needs of the victims' families were not as well looked after as they should have been.

The first day of the trial was the first time I saw the man who killed my daughter in the flesh. In fact I could hardly see him or the other defendants, as they were almost hidden behind smoked glass security screens. But from what I could see of him round the sides of the screens he looked, frankly, like nothing. I felt no great rage or hatred. I just thought he was an insignificant individual.

At times my son had looked through the security glass at the dock and due to his eyesight he had to lean forward to gain a better look. One of the defendants complained to the court that he was being intimidated! How pathetic can you get? It was another piece of evidence that these men are just the dregs of society. All they could think about was their 'rights'. What about Nicola's and Fiona's rights? What about their right to life? What about their rights in court? We were there to represent them because they could no longer represent themselves. I feel that if you have pleaded guilty to a crime you should lose your rights to dictate how the trial is run. It's the victims' rights that should matter.

The trial slowly ground into action, starting with the evidence concerning the murder of Mark Short in the Cotton Tree, and we sat through the initial statements. Cregan pleaded not guilty to all the offences. Somehow he must have imagined that a jury would believe, in the face of all the evidence, that he had not intentionally killed anyone. One part of his defence was going to be a claim that the gun had gone off accidentally. What - sixty-odd times?

Everyone was expecting the trial to last for months, but late on day four there was a dramatic development. The court was told that Cregan had changed his plea on the charges of murdering Nicola and Fiona to guilty.

It's not quite clear why he changed his mind. It may be because he was hoping for a lighter sentence, but there has been a suggestion that the interviews he'd had with a psychiatrist and psychologist in prison had revealed embarrassing personal information, and if he had continued to deny the murders this evidence would have been heard in court. As John Scheerhout put it in his book, 'Prison is an unforgiving environment at the best of times. It cannot be any better if the world knows your sexual foibles or that you are a bed-wetter. For a macho man like Cregan, reputation was all important'.

The trial continued of course, as in any case he was still denying the killings of Mark and David Short.

Some of the evidence was very hard to take. When they played the CCTV footage of Nicola and Fiona getting in the van at Hyde police station it was quite harrowing. That was the last time we or anyone else saw them alive and carefree. It was like watching a live TV show. You expect a big policeman to get into one of those vans and there was Nicola's slim form, and she had no idea what she was going into. She did a perfect three-point turn, then out through the car park barrier and on to the road. It was so difficult to watch knowing what the ending would be, again like watching a TV show - you want to stop it or change the ending, but obviously you can't. Nat said she had felt like rushing out and shouting 'Nicola stop, don't go!' Fortunately they didn't release that footage to the press. It was unbelievably upsetting, to see my daughter innocently going off to her death like that.

The van's route was followed on a series of traffic cameras as it turned out on to the M67 and headed for Hattersley. It was last picked up driving past the Tesco store on the Hub in Mottram, half a mile from their destination. They must have turned off down the

Stockport Road and left into Ashworth Lane before finally turning into Abbey Gardens. Then minutes later the same cameras showed the stolen blue BMW tearing past on the reverse journey – again so difficult to watch knowing what had happened in between. He drove at reckless speeds though residential areas, knowing full well that there were probably several ARVs (Armed Response Vehicles) on the way to find him and no doubt fully aware of what the consequences of being stopped by them would be. He would probably not have got out of the car alive.

I got intensely irritated at one point by the tapping of journalists immediately behind us as they tweeted and texted on their phones. They were only doing their job, but it was quite trying. There were constant taps and buzzes and beeps from behind us.

Before the end of the trial we agreed to complete some 'pooled' press interviews that would be released once sentencing had occurred. This took place in the music room at the Police Training Centre, Sedgley Park, where Nicola had done so much of her training and where just three years previously I had taken the photograph that was released at the time of her death.

During the interviews with TV, radio and newspaper journalists we were accompanied by the GMP Press Officer, my Deputy Governor, Mark Hanson, and one of the FLOs. We had again been briefed by the Prison Service Press Office regarding boundaries and guidelines. Each of the interviewers had been given the same brief, but it didn't prevent one of the journalists who was recording what I was saying on her mobile phone from constantly moved the microphone closer and closer. I thought, any minute now I'm going to ram that microphone up your backside. Then she asked 'What do you think about Cregan and what might happen to him?' the Press Liaison Officer and Mark jumped up and stopped her, saying, 'You've had the brief!' Later the news editor said it was a mistake, but of course it wasn't, it was obviously deliberate, a deliberate mistake if you like.

One by one Cregan's former friends turned against him in the courtroom, telling the court that he had acted on his own. No honour among thieves, of course. Leon Atkinson, who had been his friend for eight years, called him a 'lunatic'. Their pathetic attempts to get themselves off the hook and put it all on him all failed, because their stories were so confused and implausible and there was just too much evidence against them.

Later Cregan decided to admit to the murders of the Shorts as well. By now he had told everyone except the court that he was guilty - the psychiatrist and psychologist, his mother and his co-defendants, as well as of course the officer he had handed himself into. The fact that he had murdered Short, according to the Crown's QC, Nicholas Clarke, was 'the worst-kept secret in Strangeways'.

All Cregan's QC could do was invite the clerk of the court to put the charges to the defendant again and listen to his client change his plea to guilty to all of them, except for one of the attempted murder charges.

It wasn't until four months later that the whole ordeal came to an end, on the 77th day of the trial. On the day of sentencing, June 13 2013, we were all sitting waiting in a conference room at a hotel across from the court building, where we had sat waiting day in, day out for two weeks. As lunchtime approached we decided to head into the town for some lunch.

Sam and I had just sat down in a restaurant after ordering our food when my phone rang. It was to tell me that the jury was about to return to court, so we immediately rushed back to the hotel and changed back into our 'court' clothes. Then we charged back to the court building, but after all that the jury weren't quite ready yet. In fact it was about half past one by the time they finally came back into court.

Although of course there was no doubt about the outcome, it was still a very tense moment. I just wished it could have been dealt with more quickly. It seemed to go on for ever, with all the pomp and circumstance.

John Scheerhout says in his book that Cregan asked his barrister to tell the court that he wished he had killed more people while he had had the chance. This request was declined and his counsel did not enter any plea of mitigation.

Once the jury had confirmed their verdict, there was a long summing-up from the judge. He didn't address the man in the dock as 'Mr Cregan' any more - it was just 'Cregan'.

'You acted with premeditated savagery' he told him. 'You drew those two officers into a calculated trap for the sole purpose of murdering them in cold blood.'

The judge turned to the victim impact statements that we and Fiona's parents had prepared for private use by the court. 'The statement spells out the reality... of the grim duty of identifying the body of a child or loved one... the reality of living as a parent bereaved of a child, noting as the years go by each anniversary or event which the deceased child had not lived to enjoy.'

Handing out six life sentences, the judge told him that in such exceptional circumstances, a sentence of life imprisonment meant a 'whole-life tariff'. Cregan would never be released from prison.

Paul Bone has stated that he believes the murder of an officer of the law on duty should be punishable by the death penalty. It is hard not to sympathise with his view.

Outside the court, I gave a statement to the press:

'Nicola left home for work that morning like any other morning, in the expectation that she would return home at the end of her shift. We were ripped apart beyond belief that day. Nothing could have prepared us for the utter devastation we were about to endure, for no other reason than the fact that Nicola was a police officer. She was brutally and callously murdered in the most despicable and cowardly way. We can only imagine what thoughts and feelings she experienced in those few seconds it took for this person to pull the trigger and for Nicola to draw her last breath.

'Our lives have been shattered beyond belief and we will never be the same again. To have a child taken away from you in such a cruel and meaningless way is without doubt the worst thing any parent can imagine. The number of people affected by Nicola's death is a measure of how popular and loved she was by her family, friends and colleagues alike.

'There are other people who should also bear some responsibility for the deaths of Nicola and Fiona, those who harboured and assisted this person while he was at large.

'It is beyond our understanding how and why anyone could want to murder two innocent young women who were doing their jobs and had arrived with nothing but thoughts of providing assistance to someone in need of their help. Our whole lives will always surround what happened on that day. Birthdays, Christmas and anniversaries are now lost to memories and will never be the same again. Our lives will always be empty without Nicola.'

I still feel exactly the same way.

CHAPTER 7

'Don't ask me how I am, just tell me you're pleased to see me'

The day after the trial ended, I felt completely exhausted. I didn't know which way was up. I felt as if I had flown the Atlantic ten times without stopping. When I finally woke up, I had a terrible sense of anti-climax. That was one day when I could have done with the support of the family liaison officers, but as it happened they were both away. It does help more than you'd imagine just to have someone knock on the door and say, 'How are you feeling, do you want a cup of coffee?' But we did get a lot of thoughtful text messages and phone message asking if we were OK. Of course we weren't OK, but it always helps to know that there are people around who care.

All I could think of straight after the trial was that we needed to go shopping. Every time I had walked into a supermarket over the past few months I had seen see my daughter's picture on the front pages of the newspapers. I thought, 'the joke's over now, let's go back to normal', but of course it wasn't, there were still great big pictures of her everywhere. One newspaper had a huge photo of Cregan next to a picture of Nicola - I felt that was just wrong, as if they were equivalent to each other in some way. And all the headlines said 'read all about it on pages 2, 4, 5, 6, 7 and 8' and so on. I kept imagining Nicola walking in and saying 'that's been a tough couple of years then, Dad' in the way she would do. It was still hard to believe I would never see her again. It still is. It always will be.

I worry so much at times that I will forget what she looks like, what she smells like and even worse what her voice sounds like.

One effect of the trauma was the loss of my short-term memory. I had always prided myself at work on remembering every internal phone number and knowing all the mobile phone numbers of people I rang regularly. Now I found I had forgotten them all. Yet having a good memory for events had become my worst enemy, because I just couldn't stop thinking about

Nicola and remembering what had happened to her and how I had last seen her. As I put it in a press statement, it was like a nightmare you can never wake up from.

I found people's reactions quite hard to take sometimes. Some people would just avoid eye contact or change direction so as not to have to talk to me. Or they would say, 'I know it's a silly question, but how are you feeling?' Well - it is a silly question! It feels as if they all have the same cue card and they pass it from one to the other. What do they expect me to say? Some people would say nothing, just give me a pat on the back and move on. That's fair enough. I do understand it's difficult for people to know what to say. If people are wondering what to say, I would suggest: 'Don't ask me how I am, just tell me you're pleased to see me'.

At one point the BBC programme *Crimewatch* wanted to do a tribute programme combined with a reconstruction of the crime. I felt there was no point – it's not as if there was a criminal to be caught. So we said no. The media can be so insensitive. When that magazine office in Paris was attacked by terrorists in January 2015, the media showed actual footage of a police officer being shot dead. That's incredibly insensitive, what would that have been like for the relatives? You can't help imagining what it would have looked like when Nicola and Fiona were shot.

It's funny how you become sensitive to certain words which connect you to what happened. We can't watch programmes about crime or violent films on the TV any more. There was one drama we nearly saw about a policeman being killed and another about a sniper murdering a police officer. There was even a scene where a father answered the door to the police and said, 'Fiona's at work right now'. It seemed so insensitive, but of course I can hardly expect them to stop the way they make programmes just for us.

Just hearing the word 'gun' makes us both go cold, however innocently it's used, even if it's just a spray gun or a glue gun. Even the word 'trigger' affects me. Somebody at work made a casual remark about 'just lobbing a grenade in' to sort out a problem, and he didn't even twig what he'd said. It's the same with pictures - I get a shiver when I see photos or TV images of guns, bullets, grenades, anything like that. When we're out on the road, if an ambulance goes by with its 'blue and twos' we both sit there in silence knowing what each other is thinking, if I see a female police officer with a ponytail, I catch my breath, because it reminds me immediately of Nicola.

Nat of course has been equally devastated, although being a different personality from me she showed her grief differently.

Nat: All along the journey through what's happened to us, it's felt as if I am second best. Everyone talks about Bryn and asks how he is, not me. I want to tell them, hang on, my life's been turned upside down as well! I still have that feeling of 'where is Nicky, where did she go?' It's still impossible to believe that she has gone and I'll never see her again. I do struggle with that. It's not like losing grandparents or even parents. You're sad, especially if they're not that old, but you expect it, you know it's the way of things and that you will have to lose them eventually.

There's no way you can rationally process something like this, because what happened wasn't rational. It wasn't as if they were even trying to arrest that man. It was just random, without any reason or sense. It still freaks me out to think that he was the last person she ever saw.

Bryn and I have dealt with our grief in different ways. He has tended to face it more head on, while I need to escape from it. We don't have much of her stuff to remember her by, just her cap badge, epaulettes and ID card. We had to ask the police to send us copies of them, because they gave the originals to her mother - they didn't even think that we might have liked them. I have kept a box of Nicola's personal things, and if I feel I want to be near her I sometimes put her hoodie and socks on or wear her Britney Spears perfume.

I tend not to deal with big problems head on, I usually avoid them. Bryn has dealt with it by doing all his amazing charity work in her memory, but I find it really hard to get involved in that because it's a reminder every day and I need to be able to stop thinking about it. When the charity was based at home you couldn't escape it.

We didn't know which way to go at first, what to do with ourselves, because we were being stage managed all the time by the police. You keep playing it over again and again in your head. I was talking to somebody a while ago who had a relative who was dying of cancer, and I thought 'you selfish man, at least you're going to get the chance to say goodbye, that's more than we had'. Not fair really, but that's how it feels. So most of the time I don't think about it.

After it happened, all these people were suddenly my best friends and constantly texting and ringing, but then after a few weeks there were just a few left who were still bothering, and they weren't the people you would have expected. In fact I have made some friends as a result of all this. I have five amazing new friends I would have never have met otherwise, and they have helped me so much. At least it's good to think of the wonderful things that have happened because of Nicola.

Trying to sort out practical things like closing her Facebook account gave me things to do, and I was quite focused, but after a couple of days Bryn was the one who was together and I was the one who was a wreck. That first Christmas was really difficult. All the time when I was Christmas shopping, I kept seeing things in the shops and thinking, oh, Nicky will like that, and then remembering that she wasn't going to be here.

Going back to work has been my saviour. I went back to my job at Wakefield Prison after the trial ended, at the end in January 2014. I worried that I wouldn't be able to handle it because I wouldn't be able to separate what happened to Nicola from my job, but thankfully that hasn't been the case.

I do think too much - I ruminate all the time. I have an irrational obsession with the idea that you might go to work and never come home, the way Nicola did.

The last thing we wanted after the trial was to sit around and think about things. A couple of days after it finished, we went for a three-day break to Thorpe Park at Windsor, as Nat and 1 both like theme park rides - we're adrenalin junkies on the quiet. Before the actual trial we decided to get away and fly to Florida for a week and had some 'fun' in Disneyland, but we were unable to relax because of the intrusive thoughts which kept affecting us at times.

Not surprisingly, my health wasn't doing too well with all this and one day I was hit by a terrible pain in my stomach. When I went to the doctor he took a quick look at me and picked up the phone to the hospital to book me in as an emergency. At first it was thought I had ruptured my appendix, so I was rushed into theatre at 11 o'clock at night. In fact it wasn't my appendix - it turned out it was an inflamed bowel, brought about through the stress I'd experienced.

That night in my hospital bed I heard the church clock as it chimed every quarter right through the night. Every time I closed my eyes I could see Nicola coming towards me in her police uniform, I could hear her voice and smell her perfume. It seemed so real, and then it was so cruel when I awoke to find that it wasn't real.

The following morning the consultant came around along with some student doctors. They were looking at possible causes for my condition and finally got to stress. He asked me if anything stressful was going on in my life. I told him what had happened, and I could see tears streaming down a couple of faces.

Unfortunately Sam took a long time to recover. After the trial finished he spent the first 48 hours in bed, only waking up for about two hours. After that he stayed in bed for days at a time. He really hit rock bottom, getting drunk every night, and struggled to pick himself up. As he put it, he had never had to deal with stress before and he had no idea how to cope. He couldn't find a way to express or handle his anger. It didn't help that he lost his job teaching PE in schools because of the time he had to take off work, which was a great shame. He was on a zero hours contract, so they gave him zero hours work. It's shameful how an employer could treat someone like this.

Sam has reached some low points, he won't mind me saying, but I'm pleased to say he did finally admit that he needed help. He didn't want to tell me how he was feeling because he didn't want me to worry.

Everyone is affected differently. My mother, who is now 75, is from a generation where you don't go to the doctor unless you have a real physical illness, so she's reluctant to look at bereavement counselling or anything like that. She has dealt with it all in her own way, by making a little shrine to Nicola, and she buys flowers for it every week.

When Nicola worked in the shoe shop she bought her a pair of boots after her Nan slipped in the snow about five years ago, and my mum treasures them and keeps them resoled and heeled - echoes of Trigger's broom from 'Only Fools and Horses' which has had three new heads and two new handles! The last time she took them to Timpsons they suggested it was time to throw them away, but she wouldn't hear of it. Because Nicola gave them to her, she'll keep them for ever.

I returned to work in the months before the trial, really to give myself something to do. My boss was brilliant. She said to me, 'Take it day by day. If you want to come in, come in, and if you don't, then don't. If you want to, ring me, whatever you want.' In a way she was saying 'You've got a big decision to make here, don't make the wrong one'. That's not the sort of consideration you'd normally expect in the prison service and I feel I was lucky to have such an understanding boss.

It wasn't just family who were affected. Nicola's boyfriend Gareth was serving with the specials, but he has never put on a uniform again since that day. One of the two police officers who were first on the scene hasn't been able to return to work.

Chief Superintendent Nick Adderley told John Scheerhout of the *Manchester Evening News*: 'The reality is that these officers are never likely to return to front-line duties again. They continue to be supported by the force.'

In a special edition of 'Brief', the Greater Manchester Police magazine, he wrote:

'They say, look beyond the uniform of every police officer and you see an ordinary person doing an extraordinary job. Nicola and Fiona were ordinary young women doing an extraordinary job in an exceptional way...

'Nicola was one of those officers who I would say every team needs. She was great at her job, full of beans, had a great sense of humour and was a real joy to be around. In her application form to the police, Nicola wrote that she wanted to make a difference, that she wanted to make her family proud and that she wanted to change the image of the police by being the very best she could be. Without any doubt Nicola achieved every ambition she set out on her form.

'Words cannot describe the sadness and sense of loss the Division feels, and my heart goes out to the incredible families of both Nicola and Fiona, as their sense of loss must be many times that of ours.

'At 10.53 on Tuesday 18 September, Police Constable Fiona Bone and Police Constable Nicola Hughes faced evil head on. They did not run, they did not hide, they did not cower and allow evil to prevail. They stood tall and delivered against the very statement of the oath they swore when they became police officers. We will never forget the sacrifice our officers gave, but more importantly we will never forget Nicola and Fiona, as people, as teammates and as beacons of all that is great about British policing.'

Returning to work was a difficult decision to make, as my attitude had changed. Previously I would attend MAPPA (Multi Agency Protection Panel) meetings, but now I thought, I can't do this. I couldn't get involved talking about the various things prisoners had done, which obviously included murder. I was becoming more aware that I didn't want to have contact with prisoners any more. My attitude to them had changed, and I couldn't change it back. I didn't even want to talk to inmates I had known for 15 years or more and was on first-name terms with. I was thinking, 'I don't want to be around people like that, I don't want to be talking to them any more'.

At one point when I had returned to work a prisoner who I had known for years approached me to offer his condolences, and I just said to him, 'I can't speak to you'. He thought I meant I was too busy to stop and talk, but his crime was murder, and that was just too close to home for me.

In the old days I would have been aware of what these men had done, but I'd be able to detach myself and not think about it. Now it was different, because I knew exactly what their victims' families were going through and I couldn't just treat them as normal people any longer. If one of them had said the wrong thing, he could have ended up wearing my extendable baton. You can't do a prison officer's job if you're feeling like that.

I hadn't been planning to retire yet, not at 51 after only 25 years - I was supposed to retire at 60 and enjoy retirement. But I knew I'd had enough. I found myself thinking too much about the crimes prisoners had done, watching them walk across the yard. Suddenly, what they were inside for had begun to matter to me personally. I couldn't keep the emotional detachment any more. You read all the horrifying details, but you learn to forget it and think about something else. If you started thinking about it you'd go out of your mind.

Before losing Nicola I remember explaining how I dealt with the job when people asked me how I managed to work in a prison. They said 'how do you work in here?' and I told them you don't focus on it. You develop an outer shell of resilience which enables you to go to work every day, but now that shell had cracked and I knew it couldn't ever be fixed.

Being a prison officer is no picnic. I've seen prisoners who have committed suicide, dealt with cell fires, been assaulted and had buckets of urine and excrement thrown at me. I've been subjected to every insult under the sun. I've been stabbed in the arm with a homemade implement, I've had teeth knocked out.

You don't always see it coming. One Christmas Day I found a prisoner watching the Queen's Speech on the TV and I said 'You know you can't watch this'. As I turned away I suddenly heard the sound of the TV getting louder. It was flying through the air at me - he had picked it up and thrown it across the room.

I've walked into the unit and found it smashed up, all the furniture broken and glass on the floor. I've dealt with dirty protests and had to wear protective clothing just to give prisoners their meals. Recently I gave a speech at the Prison Officers' Conference where I said that if you lived in an area where that sort of thing happened you would soon put your house up for sale, but we prison officers have no choice, we have to go on with it every day.

So I packed it all in in September 2014, two years after Nicola had died. I miss my colleagues and all the comradeship and banter. I still get people saying 'When are you coming back?' when they see me.

Looking back over the last three years, would I handle it all differently? Yes, I would want to make some changes. I would want more control, and I would be more forward about asking for my feelings to be taken into account. There is room for quite a few changes in the way victims of crime are dealt with. There were times when I think people assumed that because of the job I did and being close to the police, I would find it easier to handle. That's not the case.

I'd like to think the person who killed my daughter is not having too easy a time in prison. You wouldn't be human if you didn't think that. I heard he went on hunger strike because he wanted to be nearer to his family - my heart bleeds! I find it hard to accept that anyone who has committed such a brutal, calculated crime should still have the same human rights as the rest of us.

It's some comfort that he's been given a whole life tariff, but who knows what might happen to him in 30 years' time? The law might change.

Apparently one in four parents who have lost their children through murder never work again, and one in five develop a dependency on alcohol. That's a shocking statistic. The death of a child is also a major factor in divorces. We need to do more to help people who suffered this way to get their lives back.

CHAPTER 8

Remembering Nicola

In the aftermath of the crime, flowers, messages and cards came pouring in. So did donations. We all chose three charities to receive the money. One was the North West Benevolent Fund, which raises money to help police officers and their families in time of crisis, while the other was COPS (Care Of Police Survivors), which is dedicated to helping the families of officers who have lost their lives in the line of duty to rebuild their lives. The third was Victim Support.

Charity events in honour of Nicola and Fiona began almost immediately. In November 2012, Metropolitan Police officers and police staff took part in a 190-mile bike ride from London to Manchester, finishing at GMP headquarters. The event raised around £9000.

There have been various suggestions for ways of remembering Nicola and Fiona. Within a few months of the murders, a memorial garden was unveiled in the grounds of Hyde Police Station. The idea is to provide a long-lasting tribute to them and a place of quiet contemplation and reflection for friends and colleagues. It was created with the help of sponsorship money from local people and businesses.

As the fundraising grew, I felt I needed focus and drive in life, so I decided to raise money for the three charities mentioned. As part of this fundraising, in the winter of 2013 we announced 'Run to Remember', a national police force running challenge, as our first fundraising project. I asked for 10 officers from every police force in the country to run two miles a day for 125 days, making a total of 250 miles each, with the aim of raising £100 each, which across the country would have added up to £43,000. At first we had a couple of hundred, then 500, then 1000 signed up, and still they kept coming. In the end we got almost 2000 officers to take part and many of them raised a lot more. We actually raised well over £50,000. People in forces in other countries heard about it and joined in too, even from Canada and Australia.

We thought a lot of people would drop out, but around 90 per cent of those who said they would do it actually saw it through, even though many of these people were not runners at all. It was for all comers, not just keep-fit types. People built up their mileage by walking at first before going on to running. People were losing weight, getting fit and reducing their blood pressure, so it did some good all round. They told us we had inspired them.

The idea was for everyone to start off their first run at the same time, 12 noon on 1st Dec 2013, wherever you were. We had BBC and ITV coverage for the first run. After that, for the next 125 days they did their running whenever they wanted. It just grew and grew. A certain retail sports chain must have made a fortune!

We decided that each Sunday would be a themed run where runners would take pictures of themselves, one week was superheroes, one officer did the run in uniform because she said her son had called her a hero and was proud of her job. Another did it for her dad, who had been fighting cancer. The final Sunday was on the first day of spring, so the theme for the day was a clock face - wherever you went you had to get a photo of a clock. The idea was that the clocks were going forward, just as we had all moved forward. Those of us that are left have the luxury of time, something those who have died have no more of.

Following on from this we decided to establish a charity in Nicola's name and memory, a charity dedicated to providing help to youngsters who had suffered the loss of a close family member through violent crime. That's how the PC Nicola Hughes

Memorial Fund was born. It was created to provide learning opportunities and pre-employment skills in the form of support through grants or services to youngsters under 21 who have lost a parent through crime. This experience obviously has a devastating effect on adults, but it has an equally devastating effect, if different, on children.

The aim is to help them to try and rebuild their lives and look towards the future and to help them to stand on their own feet by continuing with education, perhaps if there is less money following the death of a parent, or start a course that will enable them to gain employment. We chose a butterfly design for a logo, partly because Nicola had worn a butterfly necklace for years - she always seemed to be wearing it - and also as a reference to the 'butterfly effect' developed by Edward Lorenz. In chaos theory, the butterfly effect is a 'sensitive dependence on initial conditions' in which a very small change can lead to a significantly different outcome at a later date. So we're hoping that by making a small change we can achieve something much bigger in the future.

CHAPTER 9

The North Pole Marathon

My next 'good idea' was to take part in the North Pole Marathon, organised by Richard Donovan. I had watched a documentary months before we lost Nicola about 'the world's coolest marathon', which has taken place each April since 2006. Only 50 people are allowed to take part each year and apparently fewer than 400 people in the world have ever completed it - Richard was the first.

The race takes place literally at the North Pole, in temperatures down to minus 40 degrees. The course is a full marathon distance of 26.2 miles, made up of 10 laps of a 2.6 mile circuit. You run entirely on ice, the frozen surface of the Arctic Ocean. You have a few feet of ice underneath your feet, and below that there's nothing but 12,000 feet of ocean.

The men's record is just over three and a half hours, which would be a pretty respectable time for a normal marathon, but most times are much slower than that for obvious reasons, as you very quickly get covered in frost and start to suffer from chill, however well you cover yourself up.

I wondered who would be stupid enough to join me in this crazy fundraising project so I invited a friend, Rob Stapleton – sorry Rob! - who at the time trained at my karate club and is a serving GMP Officer. Rob wanted to help me raise some money in memory of Nicola, our target being £50,000.

Once we had decided to enter and confirmed things with Richard Donovan we embarked upon an intensive training programme. With barely 12 months to prepare for it, we had a steep hill to climb. We had so many things to organise, including fundraising, sponsorship, flights and accommodation, while at the same time we had to start running.

Our training usually consisted of a five-mile run near to the karate club, uphill for most of it, and we then progressed to the local reservoir in Dovestones, Saddleworth. The distance around the reservoir was exactly 2.6 miles, which replicated the distance around the North Pole. Our intention was to build up the laps in preparation for the marathon.

At times we were joined by other members of the karate club, who probably thought we were stupid. More than likely they were correct, but it was giving me some much-needed focus and I was able to channel all my grief and anger into preparing for it.

We needed to experience the harsh weather that Saddleworth usually throws at you during winter, but we were disappointed to experience one of the mildest winters in years. Other methods were needed. We contacted the indoor ski slope in Manchester, Chill Factore, who allowed us to run up their indoor slope a few times at minus 4 degrees. This still wasn't quite what we needed, so I contacted the Sports Science Dept at Leeds Metropolitan University and was referred to Dr Ben Jones and his team including Louise, Lauren, Costas and Suzi. They proved more than willing to look at two middle-aged non-athletes who were trying to turn themselves into polar marathon runners. Imagine the challenge to them!

So after an initial health screening and various tests, we embarked upon a cold weather acclimatisation training plan in the 'chamber' at Leeds University. Every day for two weeks we travelled across the M62 to dress in our Arctic running gear and enter the chamber for up to two hours at a time at temperatures of minus 25.

We would take it in turns to run on the treadmill or cycle on the stationary bike. Every 15 minutes we would swap over, but not before we had our fingers pricked and a blood sample taken to measure blood sugar levels etc. At the end of those two weeks every finger on both hands had numerous holes in them. I donate blood regularly, but I was tired of that needle by the end of two weeks.

We were also required to keep a food diary for the month prior to the run, but I'm sure Rob wasn't entirely honest, especially when it came to how many pints of Guinness he had consumed!

Soon the departure date was looming and we made our final check of our donated equipment:

- North Face parka for wearing during 'down time'.
- Keela outer shell jacket and trousers to wear while running.
- Armadillo merino wool base layer, socks, gloves and beanies.
- Rudd snow chains for additional grip while running.
- Bolle goggles, which proved ineffective due to the sweat freezing inside, although that was no reflection on the product.

The rest of the clothing was made up of usual hoodies etc.

Our expedition started on Sunday 6th April 2014 with us flying from Manchester Airport to the remote island of Svalbard in the Arctic Circle. We were accompanied by a young reporter from ITV Granada, Adam McClean. Adam had been involved with new coverage about Nicola from the day it all happened back in September 2012. Since that week we spent in the Arctic we have become good friends, and Adam has since become a member of our charity panel as a media advisor. Friendships are formed in circumstances like that.

However it wasn't all plain sailing for Adam, who of course came with a strict budget from ITV. I'm not sure who set the budget but they cannot have been aware of the high prices on the island of Svalbard, because Adam blew the entire budget plus more and was subsequently sent on a budget management course!

Adam won't mind me saying that he was a little naïve at times. When we landed in Oslo and were waiting for our connecting flight, Jim Cook, the ITV cameraman, and I told Adam that all the camera equipment (which he had just paid over £1,000 excess baggage allowance for) had been put on a flight to Iceland instead, and he believed us. I knew from that moment we could have some fun with him.

During the first few days in Svalbard we filmed a number of hours of interviews to use in the three-part report planned for our return. We were filming on an area of land at the edge of the sea, which was of course frozen. Nearby was a road sign stating that the land was a breeding ground for Arctic terns and that if they flew towards you, you should take one of the red plastic poles and hold it above your head to discourage them. Of course I told Adam that the poles were to be used in the event that you were attacked by a polar bear, and because they were colour-blind like bulls they would chase the stick when you threw it for them. This was compounded by the fact that Adam wore a bright red coat for the entire trip! Needless to say he bought it, and held onto the stick for some time until I told him we were pulling his leg.

As part of the filming we obviously came up with some 'out takes' and we filmed a spoof version of this scene, all available to see on our website.

We flew up to the actual North Pole on Tuesday 8th April in an AN-74TK-100 Antonov jet, a converted cargo plane purpose-built for the conditions. We flew to Ice camp Barneo, which lies between 89N and 90N, drifting in the high Arctic Ocean. The flight duration was 2½ hours each way. The Antonov is a medium-sized transport aircraft, and its unique design makes it perfect for hostile weather conditions and shorter landing strips.

Stepping off the plane at the Pole was like nothing I had ever imagined or experienced. I have obviously never been to the Moon, but I can imagine that it is not dissimilar. I recall that once we landed Ferghal Murphy, Richard's assistant, said 'welcome to the polar ice cap'. It was like a scene from Ice Station Zebra or a Bond film, with Ferghal stroking a cat and saying, 'Welcome to the polar ice cap, Mr Bond'.

Once the door opened you could feel the icy draught in a temperature of around minus 32. I had never experienced cold like that and was glad we had spent that two weeks in the almost balmy minus 25 at Leeds University.

We were given a briefing by the Camp Commander, a Russian military type, who told us where we could and couldn't go around the camp, including the area reserved for Russian Special Forces training. We were alerted to the lack of en suite toilet facilities in our tent and pointed to the one Portaloo which would be used for all 50 men and women, women for both functions but men for number two only, he said. If you needed a pee there were strategically placed oil drums for this!

The run started at 11 am the following day after very little sleep in the 24 hours of daylight. The temperature was hovering around minus 32 when we set off, although it was nearly midday!

Richard had told us earlier that because of the snow not compacting and the bad conditions, it was necessary to reduce the lap distance, but increase the number to 12 laps to compensate. WHAT? We had only trained for 10 laps, so psychologically this was a devastating piece of news.

We all set off down the compacted runway for the first 800 metres, thinking this was going to be easy, if it was like this all the way. How wrong can you be? The route was marked by flag markers which you had to keep on your left. We reached the end of the runway, turned left - and sank knee deep in snow! For the remainder of the lap it was a mixture of deep snow, crevasses, cracks in the ice and drifts of sea ice which formed a variety of mini obstacles.

Of course the elite marathon runners soon put some distance between the non-athletes among us and in fact they lapped us on more than one occasion. This added to the problems with the route conditions, as we were running in the same tracks being churned up each time a runner passed by.

We had planned to stop off in the mess tent after each lap to have a drink. We had experimented with various energy drinks at Leeds University and found that the blackcurrant flavour with hot water was the best option for taste and absorption rate. Our plan was to get in, change our frozen balaclavas, have a quick drink, then get out again within 15 minutes. It never quite worked out like that, as the other 48 runners all had the same plan and were queuing for the water boiler. This added to our planned time, which incidentally was six hours.

I did not set out on the journey for an amazing time but to finish it, for Nicola and for myself. Laps 2 to 6 were exciting, if that's the right word to use. By the time lap 7 came around I was feeling the cold and fatigue. We were now over six hours into the marathon, so our intended finish time had been and gone. The novelty was wearing off by now. The winner, Mike Wardian from the US, had finished the race in just 4 hours 7 minutes, at which point I was just over half way round. Obviously Mike is an ultra-athlete and trains expertly for events like this - unlike myself and Rob, who had eaten a 'Svalburger' in the Svalbard Lodge 12 hours previously!

As we set off for lap 7 Rob was becoming increasingly cold and tired and needed to stop off at the next lap for a rest and to get warm. I on the other hand needed to continue running, because I knew I would never get going again if I stopped. I continued alone on laps 8, 9 and 10 without a break and then stopped before lap 11 for a much-needed hot blackcurrant and energy bar.

Laps 9 and 10 were probably where I 'hit the wall', in running speak. At one point all I wanted to do was to take off my jacket and lie down behind one of the huge blocks of ice which had been formed when the waves of the Arctic Ocean had crashed into each other at the time it was beginning to freeze solid. It would have been so easy to lie down and intentionally go to sleep and not wake up. I was aware that by the time Richard and Ferghal realised I was missing it would have been too late. By now it was around 7 pm, and although it was still bright daylight the temperature had now dropped to around minus 42.

I knew full well it wouldn't have taken long before I simply froze to death. I thought it would be so quick, and I was cold anyway so it wouldn't have taken that long or been painful, and it would all be over and I would see Nicola again. No more grief or suffering from the constant ache and raw pain of missing Nicola so much. I would be nice and warm, and I would get to see Nicola again...

I had begun to slow down to a slow shuffle by this time and my feet were beginning to feel numb. Although I was wearing just one pair of Merino wool socks, up until now they had been fine. But I could feel the ice needles forcing their way down my fingers and my head was numb with the frozen sweat icicles that had formed on top of my beanie. Any minute now and I was going to lie down - the next glacier, maybe the one after? By this time the armed polar bear guards were not as much in evidence. I was alone.

But just then something else came into my head, and in my mind I could hear Nicola shouting at me. 'Come on Dadzilla, come on! Don't stop now!' she was saying. I began to think - hang on, what will happen to Nat? To Sam? To my mum? What will they think? What will the press say? I even thought how devastating it would be to both Richard and Ferghal.

So I pulled myself together, and continued to push on with tears in my eyes thinking about Nicola even more. This wasn't good, because the tears instantly froze around my eyelashes and became painful. At lap 11 I had to stop for a warm drink and prepare myself for the final push.

As I entered the mess tent Rob had just got in at the end of his tenth lap, cold and hungry. I wanted to wait, but I needed to push on, for myself and for Nicola.

With a hot blackcurrant energy drink inside me and a nice warm dry balaclava, I opened the tent door for the last time and embarked upon completing the longest and hardest thing I had ever done. I could see the end of the race - all I had to do was navigate the hundreds of flag markers that wound their way to the finish line. I thought if I never saw one of those markers again it would be too soon.

With a final spurt of exhilaration I charged over the finish line to the mass crowds that had gathered and saw Richard Donovan, Ferghal, David Wade (the official timekeeper), Mike King (photographer) and Dave Painter (cameraman). 'Well done!' said Richard as he placed my hard earned 'cold metal' medal around my neck. As I walked away from the finish line Mike King, who sadly died this year, told me not to remove my beanie because it was frozen solid and would make a great photo.

Dave Painter was filming, and he asked how I was feeling. I said that I was glad it was over and would have preferred not to have done it, but added that it was for my little girl. I was standing at the top of the world and was emotionally and physically drained beyond belief. I had finally had the chance to be alone with my thoughts and feelings and to say goodbye to my beautiful little girl who I would never see again, and it was so hard.

It was an amazing experience to do the run. I was fairly fit from regular running back home, but it was still hard going. Our intended time of six hours was nowhere to be seen, and I came over the finish line at 11 hours 6 minutes.

I worked out later that Mike Wardian usually completes marathons in 2:17, but he had completed the North Pole Marathon in 4:07. I had set out for 6:00 but came in at 11:06, so technically Mike nearly doubled his time whereas I was 54 minutes inside that (sorry Mike, but you can't argue with facts!)

At the end of the run I was absolutely starving, both with hunger and the cold. I couldn't wait to return to the mess tent for a huge bowl of piping hot chicken soup. Imagine my disappointment when I got to the tent to find the remnants in the bottom of the pan were just lukewarm dregs, with more water than pieces of chicken. I said to the Russian chef, 'could I order a fresh bowl please?' 'Nyet' came the reply. He went on to explain that the soup had been nice and hot six hours before when the main 'ultra-runners' had come in on time. So following my 11-hour marathon I sat in the mess tent with a bowl of cold chicken soup and a handful of dry biscuits – but it tasted like a five-star meal!

I returned to my tent and peeled off my frozen running gear. My fingers were numb and I was so tired now that I had stopped. Interestingly the sweat didn't smell, probably due to the low temperatures. I started to wash myself with a pack of frozen baby wipes and changed into some dry base layer clothing. Then I put my heat holder socks on and climbed into my sleeping bag. Sleep.....

About an hour later the tent door opened and Ferghal was standing there telling people that the second helicopter was leaving for the magnetic pole in 30 minutes. I had never been in a helicopter before, but I was so tired that I changed into my insulated gear and away we went in the huge Russian helicopter for the short ride north. Within minutes the majority of us had fallen fast asleep to the sound of the comforting drone of the engines and the heated cabin.

Once we landed at the magnetic pole, the pilot took out the huge symbolic red and white striped pole and located the exact point in the ice before erecting it for our joined hands 'world tour in 30 seconds' - not quite what I had ever imagined for my first round-the-world cruise!

At this point Rob began to suffer the effects of mild hypothermia due to the temperature dropping to minus 50, plus the Guinness was taking its toll from the day before...

Our return flight to Svalbard was 30 minutes shorter than the outbound flight because the ice pack had been floating south. Richard had ordered a mass pizza delivery at the Radisson for our return, and we ate like rabid dogs. It was strange, but just two hours previously we had been standing at the top of the world eating cold chicken soup and now we were in a nice warm hotel eating freshly-made pizza at 2 am in broad daylight.

Later we had the official debrief, when the winners were announced and each participant was presented with the official North Pole certificate. We were also given one of the flag markers we had been running round for 26.2 miles. At the end of the briefing Richard announced that the official race banner would be presented to one of the runners. I thought it would go to the overall winner, and I was so shocked and humbled when he announced that I would be this year's recipient. It's not often I'm lost for words, but this was one of those occasions. I struggled like hell to stop myself from becoming overwhelmed with emotion as I walked up to collect it.

Richard also then gave me the remaining 250 or so flag markers to raffle off for our charity, but I suspect he didn't want to pay the excess baggage allowance!

The next few days were spent lazing around in Svalbard waiting for the flight home. I was bored and just wanted to return home to Nat and Sam. Sam met me at Manchester Airport with Adam from ITV and a cameraman. I was nearly swallowed up by Sam's big arms, and it was a proud moment to see him again.

My plan now is to complete seven marathons in seven continents in seven years and become part of the Grand Slam Club. The next one is the New York Marathon in November 2016, with an intended finish at the South Pole in 2022.

I am currently in the early stages of planning to enter the Yukon Arctic Ultra in February 2017; this will include a team of four of us on cross-country skis for a 430-mile trek up the frozen Yukon in temperatures down to minus 50, none of us having ever been on skis before. There is lots of preparation and planning in store for us.

Before this it is my intention to take part in the New York Marathon in November 2016, partly in preparation but also to tick one more off the Grand Slam list. The Marathon Grand Slam Club comprises runners who have completed a marathon distance of 42.195 km (26.2 miles) or longer on each of the seven continents and on the Arctic Ocean at the North Pole Marathon. There are currently 63 members of the North Pole Marathon Grand Slam Club, 53 men and 10 women. To be eligible for membership, you must have completed a recognised marathon or ultramarathon on each of the continents, so hopefully I will be on the list - eventually!

CHAPTER 10

Turning horror into hope

The PC Nicola Hughes Memorial Fund

PC NICOLA HUGHES
MEMORIAL FUND
'Opportunities for the Future'

Our purpose is a simple and clearly defined one: to
make sure that the secondary victims of violent crime
don't remain victims. We honour the memories of those
who have been robbed of their lives by giving the people
touched by the loss a better life, in any way we can, big
or small. We can't prevent meaningless deaths.

We soon realised that we could continue with the fundraising, and Nat came up with the idea of establishing our own charity to focus on helping children under 21 who have lost a close family member through a violent crime such as murder or manslaughter.

We looked at how we could do this and what we could provide help for. The money isn't designed just to give kids a pleasant experience, like a holiday or a visit to Disneyland – when they return they may well have a Mickey Mouse autograph but they're still in that unfortunate position where their lifetime plans, aspirations or ambitions have been taken away from them. It would need to be something constructive that would help long term. It could be as simple as a new pair of shoes for school, or school uniform or IT equipment to enable that return to school. It could be driving lessons for a teenager so they can make their way to work, so they can earn money and stand on their own two feet. Figures would suggest that over 70% of murders in the UK involve one partner killing the other. What is usually left is the other parent in prison and children in social care or with relatives.

Nat then came up with the tag line 'Opportunities for the Future'. As the actor Sir Patrick Stewart, one of our patrons, said, the aim is 'helping them to reassemble the nuts and bolts of a normal life'.

October 2014 saw the charity directly fund three projects; firstly with Victim Support paying for the training of 92 volunteers who would be in direct contact with victims of crime, while secondly we funded the purchase of physiotherapy equipment for the North West Police Benevolent Fund to help injured police officers. Ironically this is probably where Nicola would have been helped if she had survived her injuries. Thirdly there was a ring-fenced budget for the Care of Police Survivors, for children's projects in the future.

Recently we have provided help for a number of children throughout the country whose mums have been murdered by their partners. We have provided IT equipment for several of these, which allows them to continue with study at home when they are unable to face returning to school or having 'off days'.

I received an email from one young lad whose stepdad had murdered his mum. We bought him an iPad for project work and he thanked me and asked if he was allowed to put some music on it. Little things play a huge part in their future. A donation, large or small, to the charity, or taking part in one or all of our events can be life-changing for the people we help who are affected by crime. It all helps me to feel my daughter didn't die in vain. It takes that sense of worthlessness away – I know something good has come of it. I think Nicola would approve.

We are also planning other events for 2016, including our popular annual charity ball, our Run 2 Remember 2016 and our much anticipated John O' Groats to Land's End baton relay. Details will be on our website and social media pages.

We have seen first-hand the devastating effect these deaths have on people and how we as adults cope in the aftermath, which is different from the way children cope. We continue to ask for support, however modest. Please visit our website to find out how you can help us, to contact us or to make a donation.

http://www.pcnicolahughesmemorialfund.co.uk/
Reg. charity number 1156398

CHAPTER 11

Reflections

At 10:53 am on the 18th September 2012, in a few seconds, my life changed forever. One person's decision to pull the trigger of a weapon removed any choice either Nicola or Fiona would ever have, and changed the future life choices of so many people who knew them.

My dreams of watching my young daughter grow into a beautiful young woman with a promising career in policing had been cruelly snatched away from me. Nicola's life had been so violently taken from her. My vision of planning her possible future wedding and walking her down the aisle into the arms of her intended husband was gone. The hope of seeing her have her own children, my grandchildren, was gone. The thought of Nicola being at my side when I eventually pass away would not happen. The chance to ever say goodbye was gone too.

My son Sam has been robbed of the chance to grow up with his big sister by his side. He often says 'I will never be an uncle now', and he reflected heartbreakingly upon his forthcoming 24th birthday, saying he would be older than his big sister.

The last time I saw Nicola was the evening before she died. I don't know why I drove over the Pennines to see her briefly for a few minutes but I did, and I'm so glad. She leaned into my car to kiss me goodbye, saying 'Don't get out Dad, it's cold'. If I had known that would be the last time I would see her there would have been so much I would have wanted to say to her - how proud I was of her and how she had grown into one of the wisest 23-year-olds I'm ever likely to know.

Nicola had texted me just weeks beforehand, following her attendance at a sudden death where an elderly chap had died and had been sitting in his window for several days. She had said 'Promise me if when you are old and if you are alone and I'm not there for any reason, the police won't need to force entry and find you have died alone'.

I think I replied to say 'You will always be there for me, won't you?' Nat and Nicola would often joke about how when I grew old they would look after me by making sure I went into a decent care home!

As for my future, who knows? When I'm not involved with fundraising for the charity I try to relax by watching TV. However there are certain programmes Nat and I can no longer watch because they contain so much violence and provide constant reminders and painful memories. Right now I am reading *Creative Thinking for Dummies* to try and think of some fundraising ideas! We try to have as normal a time at family celebrations as possible, but there is always something - or rather someone - missing.

We have received tremendous support from many people. We have seen people go out of their way just to offer a simple word of encouragement to other people and going to extraordinary lengths to assist in and organise charity events. Without these people we wouldn't be in the position we are in today. To them I would like to say a huge thank you. They know who they are, and they know how much I value their help and friendship.

Unfortunately there have been a couple of instances where people have behaved despicably against us for their own selfish reasons, but again if you focus on what they have done or said and get angry it's back to taking poison yourself and hoping they will suffer, when all along you're the one that suffers.

Mark Campion, an old friend and colleague who teaches mindfulness, said to me at the time that there are two things you cannot change, yesterday and tomorrow, because no matter how hard you try you can't change what happened yesterday, and no matter what you do you can't prevent tomorrow from coming.

We are doing our best to live normal lives, not just for Nicola but for each other.